STECK-VAUGHN

Math
Skills
for Life

Decimals and Percents

Harcourt Achieve

Rigby • Saxon • Steck-Vaughn

www.HarcourtAchieve.com
1.800.531.5015

Credits

Illustration Credits: Cindy Aarvig, Richard Balsam, Tami Crabb, Kristian Gallagher, David Griffin, Alan Klemp, Mike Krone, Layne Lundstrom

Photo Credits: cover b ©Mimotito/Digital Vision Royalty Free; cover c, d, g ©Sam Dudgeon/HRW; cover e ©Photos.com; p. 31 ©Stone/Getty Images; p. 47 ©Bob Daemmrich/ Stock Boston; p. 73 ©Stone/Getty Images; p. 141 ©Taxi/Getty Images.

Additional photography by Royalty-Free CORBIS and PhotoDisc/Getty Royalty Free.

ISBN 0-7398-9858-2

© 2005 Harcourt Achieve Inc.

Printed in the United States of America.

1 2 3 4 5 6 7 8 082 11 10 09 08 07 06 05 04

2

Contents

Unit 1

THE MEANING OF DECIMALS

Unit 2

ADDING AND SUBTRACTING DECIMALS

Unit 3

MULTIPLYING AND DIVIDING DECIMALS

Unit 4

RATIOS, PROPORTIONS, AND PERCENTS

Unit 5

USING PERCENTS

Unit 6

PUTTING YOUR SKILLS TO WORK

TO THE STUDENT

The four books in the Steck-Vaughn series *Math Skills for Life* are *Whole Numbers; Fractions; Decimals and Percents;* and *Measurement, Geometry, and Algebra.* They are written to help you understand and practice arithmetic skills, real-life applications, and problem-solving techniques.

This book contains features which will make it easier for you to work with decimals and to apply them to your daily life.

A Skills Inventory test appears at the beginning and end of the book.
- The first test shows you how much you already know.
- The final test can show you how much you have learned.

Most units have at least one Mixed Review and a Unit Review.
- The Mixed Review gives you a chance to practice the skills you have learned.
- The Unit Review helps you decide if you have mastered those skills.

There is also a glossary at the end of the book.
- Turn to the glossary to find the meanings of words that are new to you.
- Use the definitions and examples to help strengthen your understanding of terms used in mathematics.

Decimals and Percents Skills Inventory

Write as a decimal.

1. six hundredths 2. two and one tenth 3. two dollars 4. four cents

Change to a decimal.

5. $\frac{1}{4} =$ 6. $\frac{3}{10} =$ 7. $\frac{2}{3} =$ 8. $5\frac{1}{5} =$

Change to a mixed number or fraction. Reduce if possible.

9. .9 = 10. .01 = 11. 6.25 = 12. 12.87 =

Compare. Write <, >, or = in each box.

13. .1 ☐ .100 14. 1.3 ☐ 1.03 15. .72 ☐ .70 16. 5.6 ☐ 6.5

Round to the nearest whole number.

17. 1.3 _____ 18. .9 _____ 19. 2.51 _____ 20. 7.2 _____

Round to the nearest tenth.

21. 4.28 _____ 22. .73 _____ 23. .932 _____ 24. 17.85 _____

Round to the nearest hundredth.

25. .266 _____ 26. .019 _____ 27. 1.199 _____ 28. 5.4758 _____

Add, subtract, multiply, or divide. Round division answers to the nearest hundredth.

29.	30.	31.	32.	33.
$9.27	27.39	$5.00	95.3	7
+ 4.86	+ 11.7	− 1.49	− 1.052	− 3.68

34.	35.	36.	37.	38.
$9.25	$ .97	1.45	7.859	.2
× 8	× 100	× 8.2	× .06	× .4

39. $5\overline{)\$67.35}$ **40.** $12\overline{)\$9.98}$ **41.** $10\overline{)\$.90}$ **42.** $.7\overline{).15}$ **43.** $2.8\overline{)4.37}$

Write a ratio.

44. 5 hits and 6 misses   **45.** 10 chances in 100   **46.** two wins and two losses

Solve each proportion.

47. $\dfrac{4}{8} = \dfrac{n}{4}$ **48.** $\dfrac{2}{3} = \dfrac{4}{n}$ **49.** $\dfrac{n}{5} = \dfrac{6}{10}$ **50.** $\dfrac{1}{n} = \dfrac{5}{10}$

Write a percent using the percent sign.

51. one percent =   **52.** two and three tenths percent =

Change to a decimal or a percent.

53. $50\% =$ **54.** $205\% =$ **55.** $7\frac{1}{4}\% =$ **56.** $33\frac{1}{3}\% =$

57. $.08 =$ **58.** $.3 =$ **59.** $.75 =$ **60.** $2 =$

Change to a whole number or a fraction. Reduce if necessary.

61. $25\% =$ **62.** $7\% =$ **63.** $300\% =$ **64.** $2\frac{1}{2}\% =$

Change to a percent.

65. $\dfrac{3}{4} =$ **66.** $\dfrac{3}{100} =$ **67.** $\dfrac{1}{6} =$ **68.** $\dfrac{3}{5} =$

Compare. Use <, >, or = sign.

69.

.2 ☐ 20%

70.

70% ☐ 7

71.

$\frac{1}{2}$ ☐ 2%

72.

$33\frac{1}{3}\%$ ☐ $\frac{1}{3}$

Solve.

73.

What is 5% of 90?

74.

What is $33\frac{1}{3}\%$ of 120?

75.

What is 110% of 10?

76.

3 is 10% of what number?

77.

50 is 200% of what number?

78.

15 is $1\frac{1}{2}\%$ of what number?

79.

13 is what percent of 78?

80.

10 is what percent of 5?

Below is a list of the problems in this Skills Inventory and the pages on which the skills are taught. If you missed any problems, turn to the pages listed and practice the skills. Then correct the problems you missed in the Skills Inventory.

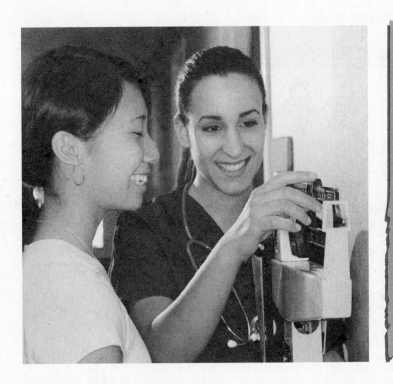

Decimals are fractions in a different form. The fraction $\frac{1}{2}$ means the same as the decimal .50. You know this because half a dollar is fifty cents or $ .50. Money and weights and measures are the most common uses of decimals.

In this unit, you will learn how to write decimals, change fractions to decimals, change decimals to fractions, round decimals, and use decimals to solve problems.

Getting Ready

You should be familiar with the skills on this page and the next before you begin this unit. To check your answers, turn to page 159.

 You can use a place value chart to help you write whole numbers.

305	three hundred five
62	sixty-two
1,324	one thousand, three hundred twenty-four

Write the following numbers in the place value chart on the right. Then write each number in words on the lines below.

1. 557   **five hundred fifty-seven** _____

2. 99 _____

3. 8 _____

4. 2,040 _____

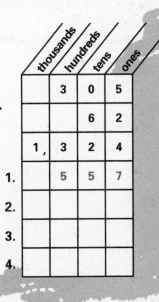

thousands	hundreds	tens	ones
	3	0	5
		6	2
1,	3	2	4
1.	5	5	7
2.			
3.			
4.			

To change a fraction to higher terms, multiply the numerator and the denominator by the same number.

Change the following fractions to higher terms.

5.
$$\frac{1}{2} = \frac{\boxed{50}}{100}$$
$$\frac{1}{2} = \frac{1 \times 50}{2 \times 50} = \frac{50}{100}$$

6.
$$\frac{3}{10} = \frac{\square}{100}$$

7.
$$\frac{4}{25} = \frac{\square}{100}$$

8.
$$\frac{3}{4} = \frac{\square}{100}$$

9.
$$\frac{2}{5} = \frac{\square}{100}$$

10.
$$\frac{13}{20} = \frac{\square}{100}$$

For review, see pages 19–20 in **Math Skills for Life, Fractions.**

 To reduce a fraction to lowest terms, divide the numerator and the denominator by the same number.

Change the following fractions to lowest terms.

11.
$$\frac{6}{18} = \frac{\boxed{1}}{3}$$
$$\frac{6}{18} = \frac{6 \div 6}{18 \div 6} = \frac{1}{3}$$

12.
$$\frac{4}{16} = \frac{\square}{4}$$

13.
$$\frac{70}{100} = \frac{\square}{\square}$$

14.
$$\frac{30}{40} =$$

15.
$$\frac{9}{27} =$$

16.
$$\frac{5}{100} =$$

For review, see pages 15–16 in **Math Skills for Life, Fractions.**

 A mixed number has a whole number and a fraction. To change a mixed number to lower or higher terms, change only the fraction.

Change to lowest terms.

17.
$$4\frac{6}{8} = 4\frac{6 \div 2}{8 \div 2} = 4\frac{3}{4}$$

18.
$$3\frac{3}{9} =$$

19.
$$1\frac{5}{25} =$$

20.
$$7\frac{10}{100} =$$

21.
$$18\frac{12}{50} =$$

22.
$$13\frac{20}{100} =$$

Change to higher terms.

23.
$$10\frac{3}{8} = 10\frac{\boxed{9}}{24}$$
$$10\frac{3}{8} = 10\frac{3 \times 3}{8 \times 3} = 10\frac{9}{24}$$

24.
$$2\frac{1}{4} = 2\frac{\square}{16}$$

25.
$$32\frac{2}{5} = 32\frac{\square}{10}$$

For review, see pages 27–28 in **Math Skills for Life, Fractions.**

Writing Decimals

Decimals are another way of writing fractions. The shaded part of each square below can be written as a fraction and a decimal.

A decimal point separates the whole number and decimal part. A decimal point is read as *and*. For example, you read 1.5 as one and five tenths.

A whole number can be written as a decimal by placing a decimal point followed by a zero to the right of the number. For example, the whole number 1 can be written as the decimal 1.0.

$\frac{1}{1} = 1 = 1.0$ $\frac{3}{10} = .3$ $\frac{7}{100} = .07$ $1\frac{5}{10} = 1.5$

one   three tenths   seven hundredths   one and five tenths

Use These Steps

Write the fraction and the decimal shown by the shaded part of the square.

1. Count the total number of parts, 10. Write 10 as the denominator.

2. Count the number of shaded parts, 1. Write 1 as the numerator.

3. Write $\frac{1}{10}$ as a decimal by writing the numerator to the right of the decimal point.

$\overline{10}$

$\frac{1}{10}$

$\frac{1}{10} = .1$

Write the fraction and the decimal shown by the shaded part of each square.

1. 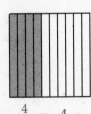   **2.**   **3.** 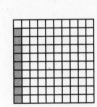   **4.**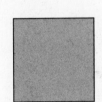

$\frac{4}{10} = .4$

Write a decimal for each fraction or mixed number.

5. $\frac{23}{100} = .23$ **6.** $\frac{9}{10} =$ **7.** $\frac{87}{100} =$ **8.** $\frac{1}{10} =$ **9.** $\frac{43}{100} =$

10. $15\frac{91}{100} = 15.91$ **11.** $4\frac{8}{10} =$ **12.** $77\frac{53}{100} =$ **13.** $6\frac{7}{10} =$ **14.** $92\frac{5}{10} =$

Changing Fractions to Decimals

It is easy to write fractions such as $\frac{1}{2}$, $\frac{1}{4}$, or $\frac{1}{5}$ as decimals. First change the fraction to a fraction in higher terms with 10 or 100 as the denominator. Then write the numerator to the right of the decimal point.

Use These Steps

Write $\frac{1}{5}$ as a decimal.

1. Multiply the numerator and denominator by 2.

$$\frac{1}{5} = \frac{1 \times 2}{5 \times 2} = \frac{2}{10}$$

2. Write the numerator, 2, to the right of the decimal point.

.2

Change each fraction or mixed number to a decimal.

1.
$$\frac{3}{4} = \frac{3 \times 25}{4 \times 25} = \frac{75}{100} = .75$$

2.
$$\frac{1}{2} =$$

3.
$$\frac{11}{25} =$$

4.
$$\frac{4}{5} =$$

5.
$$\frac{3}{20} =$$

6.
$$\frac{9}{25} =$$

7.
$$\frac{3}{5} =$$

8.
$$\frac{7}{20} =$$

9.
$$\frac{1}{4} =$$

10.
$$\frac{21}{25} =$$

11.
$$\frac{29}{50} =$$

12.
$$\frac{37}{50} =$$

13.
$$7\frac{3}{25} = 7\frac{3 \times 4}{25 \times 4} = 7\frac{12}{100} = 7.12$$

14.
$$36\frac{7}{25} =$$

15.
$$5\frac{1}{2} =$$

16.
$$1\frac{2}{5} =$$

17.
$$25\frac{3}{4} =$$

18.
$$33\frac{3}{10} =$$

19.
$$104\frac{4}{5} =$$

20.
$$90\frac{1}{20} =$$

Writing Tenths

A decimal with one digit to the right of the decimal point means tenths. For example, two tenths of a mile is written as $\frac{2}{10}$ or .2.

|◄————1 mile————►|

two tenths $=$ $\frac{2}{10}$ ◄— parts shaded $=$ .2
◄— parts in all

Use These Steps

Write five tenths as a fraction. Then change to a decimal.

1. Write the fraction.

$\frac{5}{10}$

2. Write the numerator to the right of the decimal point.

.5

Write the number as a fraction or mixed number. Then write it as a decimal.

1. one tenth
$\frac{1}{10}$ = .1

2. six tenths

3. seven tenths

4. four tenths

5. nine tenths

6. two tenths

7. seven and five tenths
$7\frac{5}{10}$ = 7.5

8. ten and two tenths

9. ninety-six and six tenths

10. nine and nine tenths

11. thirty and no tenths
$30\frac{0}{10}$ = 30.0

12. fifteen and no tenths

13. forty-two and nine tenths

14. eighty-six and three tenths

15. sixty-seven and no tenths

16. seventy and five tenths

17. six and no tenths

18. ninety-nine and no tenths

19. fifty-three and six tenths

20. twenty-one and two tenths

21. eighty and four tenths

22. thirty-two and nine tenths

Writing Hundredths

A decimal with two digits to the right of the decimal point means hundredths.

Rainfall is often measured in hundredths of an inch. Fifteen hundredths of an inch of rain is written $\frac{15}{100}$ or .15.

$$\text{fifteen hundredths} = \frac{15}{100} = .15$$

Two hundredths of an inch of rain is written $\frac{2}{100}$ or .02. Since 2 only uses one place, insert a zero next to the decimal point to fill the other place.

$$\text{two hundredths} = \frac{2}{100} = .02$$
└──── insert a zero

Use These Steps

Write six hundredths as a fraction. Then change to a decimal.

1. Write the fraction.

$$\frac{6}{100}$$

2. Write the numerator to the right of the decimal point. Since the numerator has one digit, insert a zero between the numerator and the decimal point.

.06

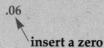
insert a zero

Write the number as a fraction or a mixed number. Then write it as a decimal.

1. seventeen hundredths
$$\frac{17}{100} = .17$$

2. twenty-six hundredths

3. eleven hundredths

4. fifty hundredths

5. ten hundredths

6. seventy hundredths

7. three hundredths
$$\frac{3}{100} = .03$$

8. one hundredth

9. eight hundredths

10. ten and twelve hundredths
$$10\frac{12}{100} = 10.12$$

11. thirty and one hundredth

12. six and no hundredths

13. ninety-nine and no hundredths

14. fifty-three and six hundredths

15. twenty-one and ten hundredths

16. eighty and fourteen hundredths

17. thirty-two and fifty-nine hundredths

Application

Decimals show parts of measures such as money, time, and weight. Sometimes you need to change part of something to a decimal. For example, thirty minutes is half an hour or .5 hours as a decimal.

Example On his timecard, Mr. Diaz needs to write in decimals the number of hours that he works. Sunday he worked $7\frac{1}{4}$ hours. What will he write on his timecard?

Change the mixed number to a decimal with two digits to the right of the decimal point.

$$7\frac{1}{4} = 7\frac{1 \times 25}{4 \times 25} = 7\frac{25}{100} = 7.25$$

Sunday	7	25
Monday		
Tuesday		
Wednesday		
Thursday		
Friday		
Saturday		

Mr. Diaz will write 7.25 on his timecard.

Change the hours Mr. Diaz worked to decimals. Complete his timecard for the week.

1. Monday Mr. Diaz worked for 4 hours.

   Answer_____

2. Tuesday he worked for $3\frac{1}{2}$ hours.

   Answer_____

3. Wednesday was his day off.

   Answer_____

4. Thursday he worked for $6\frac{1}{4}$ hours.

   Answer_____

5. Friday he worked for $8\frac{3}{4}$ hours.

   Answer_____

6. Saturday he put in $2\frac{1}{2}$ hours.

   Answer_____

Changing Decimals to Fractions

When you change a decimal to a fraction with a denominator of 10 or 100, write the digits to the right of the decimal point as the numerator of the fraction.

Notice that the number of places to the right of the decimal point is the same as the number of zeros in the denominator of the fraction.

Use These Steps

Change .08 to a fraction.

1. Write the digits to the right of the decimal point as the numerator. Omit the zero.

2. There are two places to the right of the decimal point, so the denominator needs two zeros. Write 100. Reduce.

$$.08 = \frac{8}{}$$

$$\frac{8}{100} = \frac{8 \div 4}{100 \div 4} = \frac{2}{25}$$

Change each decimal to a fraction. Reduce if possible.

1. $.7 = \frac{7}{10}$

2. $.6 =$

3. $.9 =$

4. $.1 =$

5. $1.3 = 1\frac{3}{10}$

6. $6.5 =$

7. $10.4 =$

8. $8.7 =$

9. $.57 =$

10. $.61 =$

11. $.92 =$

12. $.60 =$

13. $3.44 =$

14. $12.99 =$

15. $15.13 =$

16. $29.25 =$

17. $.05 =$

18. $.09 =$

19. $.01 =$

20. $.07 =$

21. $11.03 =$

22. $29.06 =$

23. $37.02 =$

24. $75.01 =$

25. $1.83 =$

26. $94.76 =$

27. $.45 =$

28. $25.21 =$

29. $43.66 =$

30. $6.1 =$

31. $7.2 =$

32. $9.93 =$

Money and Decimals

Amounts of money are almost always written as decimals with two places after the decimal point. For example, two dollars and fifty-nine cents is written as $2.59.

Use These Steps

Write six dollars and three cents as a decimal.

1. Write the dollar sign. Then write the whole dollar amount followed by a decimal point.

   $6.

2. Write three cents to the right of the decimal point. Insert a zero between the decimal point and the 3.

   $6.03

   ↖ insert a zero

Write each amount as a decimal.

1. seventy-two cents
   $ .72

2. nine cents

3. fifty cents

4. eighty cents

5. one dollar and one cent

6. five dollars and seven cents

7. ten dollars and forty cents

8. nineteen dollars and sixty-six cents

9. forty-seven dollars

10. twenty dollars

Write each amount in words.

11. $ .48   forty-eight cents

12. $ .92

13. $ .30

14. $ .20

15. $ .01

16. $ .05

17. $4.09

18. $11.02

19. $7.60

20. $20.10

21. $32.49

22. $75.00

Mixed Review

Write the shaded part of each square as a whole number, fraction, or mixed number. Then change to a decimal.

1.

2.

3.

Change each fraction or mixed number to a decimal.

4. $\dfrac{1}{2} =$

5. $1\dfrac{3}{5} =$

6. $27\dfrac{19}{20} =$

7. $2\dfrac{7}{10} =$

8. $\dfrac{4}{5} =$

9. $32\dfrac{7}{10} =$

10. $12\dfrac{8}{25} =$

11. $4\dfrac{87}{100} =$

12. $63\dfrac{11}{20} =$

13. $1\dfrac{9}{100} =$

14. $72\dfrac{3}{25} =$

15. $4\dfrac{9}{10} =$

Write a fraction or mixed number. Then change to a decimal.

16. six tenths

17. six hundredths

18. one and no hundredths

19. nine and one tenth

20. forty hundredths

21. fourteen and two tenths

Change each decimal to a mixed number or fraction. Reduce if possible.

22. .07 =

23. 4.5 =

24. 89.99 =

25. .33 =

26. 22.4 =

27. 69.12 =

Write each amount as a decimal.

28. two dollars

29. ten cents

30. four dollars and six cents

Write each amount in words.

31. $ .40 _____

32. $106.22 _____

Place Value

You have worked with decimals with one place (tenths) and two places (hundredths) to the right of the decimal point. The place value chart below shows decimals with three places (thousandths) and four places (ten thousandths).

six tenths

fifty-four hundredths

two hundred one thousandths

five ten thousandths

tens	ones	. tenths	hundredths	thousandths	ten thousandths
		.6			
		.5	4		
		.2	0	1	
		.0	0	0	5

Use These Steps

Write the decimal 1.306 in words.

1. Write the whole number in words. Write the word *and* for the decimal point.

one and

2. Write the decimal part. Then write the place name of the last digit.

one and three hundred six thousandths

Put each number in the chart to the right. Then write each decimal in words.

1. 60.3   <u>sixty and three tenths</u>

2. 19.7   _____

3. 1.07   _____

4. 100.11   _____

5. .89   _____

6. 2.49   _____

7. 11.299   _____

8. 99.035   _____

9. .0016   _____

	hundreds	tens	ones	. tenths	hundredths	thousandths	ten thousandths
1.		6	0	.3			
2.				.			
3.				.			
4.	1	0	0	.1 1			
5.				.			
6.				.			
7.				.			
8.				.			
9.				.			

Zeros and Decimals

You can add zeros to the right of a decimal without changing its value.

$10 = $10.00   .4 = .40 = .400

You can drop zeros at the end of a decimal without changing its value.

.500 = .50 = .5   1.000 = 1

You must *not* drop zeros in the middle of a decimal. This will change the value of the number. The symbol ≠ means *is not equal to*.

$1.05 ≠ $1.50   6.906 ≠ 6.96

Use These Steps

Decide if these decimals are equal: 1.30 ☐ 1.3

1. If there is a zero at the end of the decimal, you can drop it.

    1.3̶0̶ ☐ 1.3

2. The decimals are equal. Write = in the box.

    1.3 = 1.3

Decide if the decimals are equal. Write = or ≠ in each box.

1. $6 = $6.00

2. $1.10 ≠ $1.01

3. $4.49 ☐ $40.49

4. 5.6 ☐ 5.600

5. 17.03 ☐ 17.3

6. .8 ☐ .80

7. 100.02 ☐ 1.2

8. 209.0 ☐ 209

9. 9.9 ☐ 90.90

10. 12.300 ☐ 12.3

11. .05 ☐ .50

12. .67 ☐ .670

13. $3.90 ☐ $3.09

14. $ .79 ☐ $7.90

15. $ .99 ☐ $9.09

16. 10 ☐ 10.00

17. 30.0 ☐ 3

18. 100 ☐ 100.00

19. 8.600 ☐ 8.060

20. 35.09 ☐ 35.90

21. .550 ☐ .55

Changing Fractions to Decimals

You can change most fractions to decimals by dividing. In fact, the fractions bar shows division: the numerator is divided by the denominator.

$$\frac{1}{5} = 5\overline{)1} \qquad \frac{2}{15} = 15\overline{)2} \qquad \frac{10}{100} = 100\overline{)10}$$

Use These Steps

Change $\frac{1}{4}$ to a decimal.

1. Set up a division problem.

$$\frac{1}{4} = 4\overline{)1}$$

2. Add a decimal point and a zero. Put a decimal point in the answer above the decimal point after the 1.

$$4\overline{)1.0}$$

3. Divide until there is no remainder. Add more zeros if needed.

$$\begin{array}{r} .25 \\ 4\overline{)1.00} \\ -8 \\ \hline 20 \\ -20 \\ \hline 0 \end{array}$$

Change each fraction to a decimal using division.

1.
$$\frac{1}{5} = .2$$
$$\begin{array}{r} .2 \\ 5\overline{)1.0} \\ -10 \\ \hline 0 \end{array}$$

2. $\frac{67}{100} =$

3. $\frac{9}{10} =$

4. $\frac{3}{4} =$

5. $\frac{3}{20} =$

6. $\frac{17}{25} =$

7. $\frac{11}{20} =$

8. $\frac{4}{5} =$

9. $\frac{1}{2} =$

10. $\frac{2}{5} =$

11. $\frac{22}{25} =$

12. $\frac{4}{25} =$

13. $\frac{3}{5} =$

14. $\frac{7}{20} =$

15. $\frac{13}{25} =$

16. $\frac{37}{100} =$

Changing Fractions to Decimals

When you divide the numerator by the denominator to change some fractions to decimals, your answer may have a remainder. When this happens, write the answer with two digits to the right of the decimal point. Write the remainder as a fraction. Reduce if necessary.

Use These Steps

Change $\frac{4}{9}$ to a decimal.

1. Set up a division problem. Add a decimal point and two zeros.

$$\frac{4}{9} = 9\overline{)4.00}$$

2. Divide. Put a decimal point in the answer. You will have two decimal places.

$$\begin{array}{r} .44 \\ 9\overline{)4.00} \\ -36 \\ \hline 40 \\ -36 \\ \hline 4 \end{array}$$

3. Write the answer with two places. Write the remainder as a fraction.

$$.44\frac{4}{9}$$

Change each fraction to a decimal. Write the remainder as a fraction. Reduce if possible.

1.
$$\frac{1}{6} = .16\frac{2}{3}$$

$$\begin{array}{r} .16\frac{4}{6} = .16\frac{2}{3} \\ 6\overline{)1.00} \\ -6 \\ \hline 40 \\ -36 \\ \hline 4 \end{array}$$

2.
$$\frac{2}{3} =$$

3.
$$\frac{1}{9} =$$

4.
$$\frac{2}{9} =$$

5.
$$\frac{5}{6} =$$

6.
$$\frac{5}{9} =$$

7.
$$\frac{1}{3} =$$

8.
$$\frac{3}{7} =$$

9.
$$\frac{7}{9} =$$

10.
$$\frac{5}{7} =$$

11.
$$\frac{8}{9} =$$

12.
$$\frac{2}{7} =$$

Comparing Decimals

To compare decimals, line up the decimal points. Start at the left, and compare the value of the digits in each place. The greater number is the number with the greater digit farthest to the left.

Use the symbol < for *less than*.
Use the symbol > for *greater than*.

Comparing decimals is easier if both decimals have the same number of places. Add zeros to the end of the decimal if needed.

Use These Steps

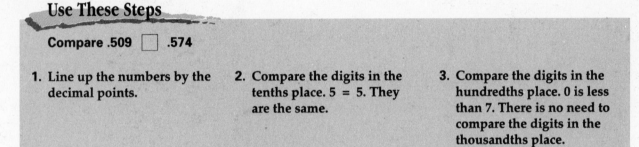

Compare .509 ☐ .574

1. Line up the numbers by the decimal points.

2. Compare the digits in the tenths place. 5 = 5. They are the same.

3. Compare the digits in the hundredths place. 0 is less than 7. There is no need to compare the digits in the thousandths place.

.509
.574

.5 09
.5 74

.5 0 9
.5 7 4
0 < 7, so .509 < .574

Compare the following decimals. Write >, <, or = in each box.

1. .73 < .83
   .7 3
   .8 3

2. .9 ☐ .91

3. .40 ☐ .4

4. 1.362 ☐ .363

5. 25.06 ☐ 25.6

6. 9.09 ☐ .099

7. 3.42 ☐ 3.4

8. 6.92 ☐ 6.92

9. 10.1 ☐ 10.0

10. .88 ☐ .880

11. 1.033 ☐ 1.33

12. 3.30 ☐ 3.3

13. .01 ☐ .10

14. .10 ☐ .100

15. .11 ☐ 1.1

Application

Scales are used to weigh meat and produce. Electronic scales measure weight in hundredths of a pound. These scales print labels using decimals to show the net weight (Net Wt.), price per pound (Price/lb.), and the total price. The net weight is the actual weight of the food and does not include the weight of the container.

Example Mary works part-time at a grocery store. She packages meat and produce. Today she packaged $4\frac{1}{2}$ pounds of stew meat. What will the net weight read on the label?

Change the mixed number $4\frac{1}{2}$ to a decimal.

$$4\frac{1}{2} = 4\frac{1 \times 50}{2 \times 50} = 4\frac{50}{100} = 4.50$$

The label will read 4.50.

Solve.

1. Mary wrapped $2\frac{1}{4}$ pounds of ground beef. What will the net weight show on the label?

   Answer_____

2. Mary printed a label for a package of macaroni. The net weight was .9 pound. What fraction of a pound is this?

   Answer_____

3. Mary weighed out $\frac{3}{4}$ pound of strawberries. What should the label read for $\frac{3}{4}$ pound?

   Answer_____

4. The label on a bag of grapes that Mary weighed showed net weight .50. Did the bag weigh more or less than $\frac{3}{4}$ pound?

   Answer_____

5. Mary sliced and wrapped $1\frac{3}{4}$ pounds of cheese. What should the label read for $1\frac{3}{4}$ pounds?

   Answer_____

6. The label on another package of cheese that Mary wrapped showed net weight 1.65. Did the package weigh more or less than $1\frac{3}{4}$ pounds?

   Answer_____

Rounding to the Nearest Whole Number

To round a decimal to the nearest whole number, look at the digit in the tenths place. If it is less than 5, drop the decimal point and all the digits to the right.

> 2.3 rounds to 2
> .45 rounds to 0
> 17.033 rounds to 17

If the digit in the tenths place is 5 or greater, add 1 to the number in the ones place. Drop the decimal point and all the digits to the right.

> .5 rounds to 1
> 4.75 rounds to 5
> 17.622 rounds to 18

Use These Steps

Round 29.63 to the nearest whole number.

1. Look at the digit in the tenths place.

    29.6̲3

2. Since the digit 6 is greater than 5, add 1 to the whole number, 29. Drop the decimal point and the digits to the right.

    29.63 rounds to 30

Round each decimal to the nearest whole number.

1. 1.3 ___1___	**2.** 6.5 _____	**3.** 2.9 _____
4. 32.54 _____	**5.** 17.06 _____	**6.** 93.16 _____
7. 10.632 _____	**8.** 40.801 _____	**9.** 50.076 _____
10. .001 _____	**11.** .93 _____	**12.** .5 _____
13. 9.9 _____	**14.** 39.46 _____	**15.** 99.99 _____
16. 199.39 _____	**17.** 209.09 _____	**18.** 304.702 _____
19. 16.505 _____	**20.** .113 _____	**21.** 167.50 _____

Rounding to the Nearest Tenth

To round a decimal to the nearest tenth, look at the digit in the hundredths place. If it is less than 5, drop all the digits to the right of the tenths place.

.33 rounds to .3
4.446 rounds to 4.4
17.003 rounds to 17.0

If the digit in the hundredths place is 5 or greater, add 1 to the number in the tenths place. Drop all digits to the right of the tenths place.

2.56 rounds to 2.6
4.759 rounds to 4.8
.082 rounds to .1

Use These Steps

Round .693 to the nearest tenth.

1. Look at the digit in the hundredths place.

2. Since the digit 9 is greater than 5, add 1 to the digit in tenths place, 6. Drop the digits to the right.

.6<u>9</u>3

.693 rounds to .7

Round each decimal to the nearest tenth.

1.
1.73   <u>1.7</u>

2.
7.86   _____

3.
2.91   _____

4.
2.55   _____

5.
7.08   _____

6.
3.16   _____

7.
10.63   _____

8.
40.80   _____

9.
50.07   _____

10.
.051   _____

11.
.906   _____

12.
.591   _____

13.
9.970   _____

14.
39.946   _____

15.
99.999   _____

16.
199.739   _____

17.
209.099   _____

18.
999.909   _____

19.
.04   _____

20.
.011   _____

21.
1.04   _____

Rounding to the Nearest Hundredth

To round a decimal to the nearest hundredth, look at the digit in the thousandths place. If it is less than 5, drop all the digits to the right of the hundredths place.

> 2.331 rounds to 2.33
> .4846 rounds to .48
> 17.0033 rounds to 17.00

If the digit in the thousandths place is 5 or greater, add 1 to the number in the hundredths place. Drop all digits to the right of the hundredths place.

> .565 rounds to .57
> 4.7599 rounds to 4.76
> 1.0072 rounds to 1.01

Use These Steps

Round .134 to the nearest hundredth.

1. **Look at the digit in the thousandths place.**

   .134

2. **Since the digit 4 is less than 5, drop the digits to the right of the hundredths place.**

   .134 rounds to .13

Round each decimal to the nearest hundredth.

1. 7.348 _7.35_	**2.** 6.835 _____	**3.** 2.901 _____
4. 32.005 _____	**5.** 17.049 _____	**6.** 93.167 _____
7. 10.632 _____	**8.** 40.801 _____	**9.** 50.076 _____
10. .0301 _____	**11.** .9330 _____	**12.** .5555 _____
13. 8.099 _____	**14.** 39.496 _____	**15.** 99.999 _____
16. 199.3909 _____	**17.** 209.0987 _____	**18.** .9999 _____
19. 2.0041 _____	**20.** 2.0046 _____	**21.** 2.650 _____

Application

Abby works in the produce packaging department of Bert's Super Store. Her job is to inspect packages. She checks the weight of every tenth package. She compares the weight of each package to a standard weight.

Abby fills in a chart with the weight of each package. If the package weighs too much, she puts a + in her chart. If it weighs too little, she writes a − on her chart. If it weighs the same as the standard, she writes =.

Example Abby's first package of beans weighs .53 pounds. Her standard for beans is .50 pounds. Fill in the weight in the chart. Compare the weights and write +, −, or = in the chart. Write the package's weight. Line up their decimal points. Compare.

$$.5\boxed{3}$$
$$.5\boxed{0}$$
$$3 > 0, \text{ so } .53 > .50.$$

Since the package weight, .53, is greater than the standard, .50, write + in the chart.

	Example	1	2	3	4	5	6	7	8	9	10	11	12
Weight	.53	.49											
+, −, =	+	−											

Complete the chart using the package weights below.

1. .49

2. .66

3. .46

4. .39

5. .51

6. .65

7. .50

8. .44

9. .52

10. .47

11. .59

12. .64

Unit 1 *Review*

Change the fractions to decimals.

1.
$$\frac{1}{2}$$

2.
$$\frac{3}{4}$$

3.
$$\frac{3}{5}$$

4.
$$\frac{17}{25}$$

5.
$$\frac{9}{10}$$

6.
$$\frac{13}{50}$$

Write a fraction or mixed number. Then change to a decimal.

7. two tenths

8. two hundredths

9. ten and four tenths

10. four and no hundredths

11. twenty and six hundredths

Change each decimal to a fraction or mixed number. Reduce if possible.

12. .08

13. .3

14. .14

15. .27

16. 9.79

17. 10.66

18. 74.2

19. 6.5

Write these amounts as decimals.

20. ninety-five cents

21. one dollar and six cents

22. seven dollars

Write each amount in words.

23. $ .60 _____

24. $207.25 _____

25. $28.00 _____

26. $13.03 _____

Put each number in the chart. Then write each number in words.

27. 1.09 _____

28. 5.3 _____

29. 350.05 _____

30. .45 _____

31. .225 _____

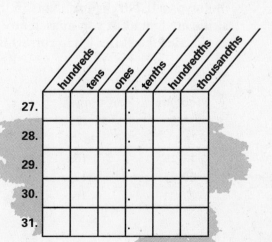

Decide if the decimals are equal. Write = or ≠ in each box.

32.
$.81 \ \square \ \$8.10

33.
400 $\square$ 400.00

34.
6.90 $\square$ 6.09

35.
$53.00 $\square$ $5.30

Change each fraction to a decimal. Write the remainder as a fraction. Reduce if possible.

36.
$\frac{4}{7} =$

37.
$\frac{7}{9} =$

38.
$\frac{1}{6} =$

Compare each set of numbers. Write =, <, or > in each box.

39.
.8 $\square$ .80

40.
.75 $\square$ .76

41.
.40 $\square$ .44

42.
33.09 $\square$ 3.309

Round to the nearest whole number.

43.
10.09

44.
7.50

45.
.59

46.
312.2

47.
784.29

Round to the nearest tenth.

48.
.95

49.
19.36

50.
109.99

51.
302.11

52.
4.14

Round to the nearest hundredth.

53.
1.001

54.
.0999

55.
3.155

56.
989.002

57.
20.101

Below is a list of the problems in this review and the pages on which the skills are taught. If you missed any problems, turn to the pages listed and practice the skills. Then correct the problems you missed in the Unit Review.

You add and subtract decimals whenever you add and subtract money. Some examples of using decimals and money are adding up purchases, counting your change from a purchase, and deciding how much more money you will need to buy something else.

Adding and subtracting decimals is the same as adding and subtracting whole numbers. You must be sure, however, to line up the decimal points so that you are always adding or subtracting digits with the same place value.

In this unit, you will learn how to add and subtract money and other decimals.

Getting Ready

You should be familiar with the skills on this page and the next before you begin this unit.

 To add or subtract whole numbers, line up the digits that have the same place value.

Add or subtract.

1.
$$462 + 22 =$$
$$\begin{array}{r} 462 \\ +\ 22 \\ \hline 484 \end{array}$$

2. $948 - 217 =$

3. $67,499 - 3,372 =$

4. $8,142 + 656 =$

5. $15,948 - 932 =$

6. $94,162 + 3,115 =$

Getting Ready

 Sometimes when adding two or more digits, the total is ten or more. When this happens, rename by carrying tens to the next column or the next place to the left.

Add.

7.
$$95 + 37 =$$

$$\begin{array}{r} 1 \\ 95 \\ + 37 \\ \hline 132 \end{array}$$

8.
$$1,147 + 283 =$$

9.
$$942 + 76 + 153 =$$

10.
$$\begin{array}{r} 39 \\ + 41 \\ \hline \end{array}$$

11.
$$\begin{array}{r} 479 \\ + \ 67 \\ \hline \end{array}$$

12.
$$\begin{array}{r} 2,431 \\ + \ \ 988 \\ \hline \end{array}$$

13.
$$\begin{array}{r} 15,889 \\ + \ 1,473 \\ \hline \end{array}$$

14.
$$\begin{array}{r} 62,437 \\ 97,563 \\ + \ 3,259 \\ \hline \end{array}$$

For review, see pages 41–44 in Math Skills for Life, Whole Numbers.

 Sometimes when subtracting, the digit you are subtracting is larger than the digit you are subtracting from. When this happens, rename by borrowing from the next column to the left.

Subtract.

15.
$$715 - 49 =$$

$$\begin{array}{r} {\scriptstyle 10} \\ {\scriptstyle 6\ \cancel{0}15} \\ \cancel{715} \\ - \ \ 49 \\ \hline 666 \end{array}$$

16.
$$436 - 55 =$$

17.
$$1,462 - 999 =$$

18.
$$\begin{array}{r} 62 \\ - 59 \\ \hline \end{array}$$

19.
$$\begin{array}{r} 837 \\ -148 \\ \hline \end{array}$$

20.
$$\begin{array}{r} 1,990 \\ - \ \ 876 \\ \hline \end{array}$$

21.
$$\begin{array}{r} 42,493 \\ - \ 1,294 \\ \hline \end{array}$$

22.
$$\begin{array}{r} 137,491 \\ - \ 42,586 \\ \hline \end{array}$$

For review, see pages 72–73 in Math Skills for Life, Whole Numbers.

 Sometimes you have to add or subtract zeros. Zero plus any number is always that number. When subtracting from a number with zero, you may need to rename.

Add or subtract.

23.
$$\begin{array}{r} 250 \\ + 300 \\ \hline 550 \end{array}$$

24.
$$\begin{array}{r} 4,700 \\ + 2,000 \\ \hline \end{array}$$

25.
$$\begin{array}{r} 50 \\ - 25 \\ \hline \end{array}$$

26.
$$\begin{array}{r} 701 \\ - \ 32 \\ \hline \end{array}$$

27.
$$\begin{array}{r} 1,000 \\ - \ \ 978 \\ \hline \end{array}$$

For review, see pages 45, 68–69, 75–78 in Math Skills for Life, Whole Numbers.

Adding Money

When you add amounts of money, be sure the decimal points are lined up. Line up the decimal point in the answer with those in the problem.

$2.39 + $8.40

$$\begin{array}{r} \$\ 2.39 \\ +\ \ 8.40 \\ \hline \$10.79 \end{array}$$

Use These Steps

Add $6.33 + $4.95

1. Be sure the decimal points are lined up.

$$\begin{array}{r} \$6.33 \\ +\ \ 4.95 \\ \hline \end{array}$$

2. Add. Begin with the digits on the right. Rename. Put a decimal point and a dollar sign in the answer.

$$\begin{array}{r} \overset{1}{} \\ \$\ 6.33 \\ +\ \ 4.95 \\ \hline \$11.28 \end{array}$$

Add. Rename if necessary.

1.

$6.75 + $2.31 =

$$\begin{array}{r} \overset{1}{} \\ \$6.75 \\ +\ \ 2.31 \\ \hline \$9.06 \end{array}$$

2. $ .40 + $ .66 =

3. $ .99 + $1.84 =

4. $ .40 + $ .95 + $1.30 =

5. $3.99 + $2.97 + $4.67 =

6. $6.69 + $4.03 =

7. $3.06 + $5.60 =

8. $7.99 + $1.99 =

9. $8.42 + $6.11 + $3.99 =

10. $1.49 + $ .99 + $4.08 =

11. $ .06 + $1.29 + $5.88 + $ .39 =

12. $2.59 + $ .95 + $ .33 + $4.41 =

Adding Money

When you add whole dollar amounts of money, include a decimal point and two zeros in the tenths and hundredths places.

$$
\begin{array}{r}
1 \\
\$39.41 \\
+\ \ \ 6.00 \\
\hline
\$45.41
\end{array}
$$

$39.41 + $6   add two zeros

Use These Steps

Add $9.09 + $17

1. Set up the problem by lining up the decimal points, one above the other. Add a decimal point and zeros.

$$
\begin{array}{r}
\$\ 9.09 \\
+\ 17.00 \\
\hline
\end{array}
$$
add two zeros

2. Add. Begin with the digits on the right. Rename. Put a decimal point and a dollar sign in the answer.

$$
\begin{array}{r}
1 \\
\$\ 9.09 \\
+\ 17.00 \\
\hline
\$26.09
\end{array}
$$

Add. Rename if necessary.

1.
$650 + $73.29 =

$$
\begin{array}{r}
1 \\
\$650.00 \\
+\ \ \ \ 73.29 \\
\hline
\$723.29
\end{array}
$$

2.
$44.40 + $7 =

3.
$760.02 + $99 =

4.
$5.99 + $19 + $400 =

$$
\begin{array}{r}
1 \\
\$\ \ \ 5.99 \\
19.00 \\
+\ 400.00 \\
\hline
\$424.99
\end{array}
$$

5.
$340 + $66.09 + $ .78 =

6.
$342.93 + $61.40 + $100 =

7.
$9 + $ .75 + $499 =

8. For his new job on the crew, Lee bought a shirt for $10 and a pair of pants for $29.99. What was the total cost of the clothes he bought?

Answer_____

9. Lee also bought a pair of work boots for $35. The sales tax was $2.80. Including the tax, how much did he spend on the boots?

Answer_____

Adding Decimals

A whole number can be written as a decimal by placing a decimal point followed by one or more zeros to the right of the decimal point.

To add decimals, line up the decimal points first. Add zeros and rename if necessary. Be sure to line up the decimal point in your answer with the other decimal points in the problem.

$8 + 2.66$

$$
\begin{array}{r}
8.00 \\
+\ 2.66 \\
\hline
10.66
\end{array}
$$
← add a decimal point and two zeros

Use These Steps

Add 1.8 + 4.25

1. Set up the problem by lining up the decimal points. Add a zero.

$$
\begin{array}{r}
1.80 \\
+\ 4.25
\end{array}
$$
← add a zero

2. Add. Begin with the digit on the right. Rename. Put a decimal point in the answer.

$$
\begin{array}{r}
1 \\
1.80 \\
+\ 4.25 \\
\hline
6.05
\end{array}
$$

Add. Rename if necessary.

1. $3 + 42.6 =$

$$
\begin{array}{r}
3.0 \\
+\ 42.6 \\
\hline
45.6
\end{array}
$$

2. $99.9 + 49 =$

3. $77.3 + 1.97 =$

4. $1 + 44.6 =$

5. $82 + 199 + 11.03 =$

6. $.001 + .01 + 1.1 =$

7. $5 + 105 + 5.01 =$

8.
$$
\begin{array}{r}
6.3 \\
+\ 7.9
\end{array}
$$

9.
$$
\begin{array}{r}
13.04 \\
+\ 6.96
\end{array}
$$

10.
$$
\begin{array}{r}
1.001 \\
+\ 9.009
\end{array}
$$

11.
$$
\begin{array}{r}
19.3 \\
+\ 24.7
\end{array}
$$

12.
$$
\begin{array}{r}
.72 \\
+\ .57
\end{array}
$$

13.
$$
\begin{array}{r}
100.3 \\
+\ 42.75
\end{array}
$$

14.
$$
\begin{array}{r}
89.73 \\
+\ 4.001
\end{array}
$$

15.
$$
\begin{array}{r}
498.032 \\
6.047 \\
+\ 10.93
\end{array}
$$

16.
$$
\begin{array}{r}
7.4 \\
7.9 \\
+\ 10.03
\end{array}
$$

17.
$$
\begin{array}{r}
143.99 \\
1.01 \\
+\ 10.
\end{array}
$$

Adding Decimals

When adding decimals, be sure to line up all of the decimal points, including the one in your answer. Rename if necessary. Add zeros to make the same number of decimal places.

$$.5732 + 19.032$$

$$\begin{array}{r} 1 \\ .5732 \\ + 19.0320 \longleftarrow \text{add a zero} \\ \hline 19.6052 \end{array}$$

Use These Steps

Add 75.0327 + 850.3

1. Set up the problem by lining up the decimal points. Add zeros.

$$\begin{array}{r} 75.0327 \\ + 850.3000 \longleftarrow \text{add three zeros} \\ \hline \end{array}$$

2. Add. Begin with the digits on the right. Rename when needed. Put a decimal point in the answer.

$$\begin{array}{r} 1 \\ 75.0327 \\ + 850.3000 \\ \hline 925.3327 \end{array}$$

Add. Rename if necessary.

1.
$$\begin{array}{r} 1 \\ .730 \\ + .079 \\ \hline .809 \end{array}$$

2.
$$\begin{array}{r} .604 \\ + 1.3069 \\ \hline \end{array}$$

3.
$$\begin{array}{r} 11. \\ + 9.309 \\ \hline \end{array}$$

4.
$$\begin{array}{r} 81.1055 \\ + .34 \\ \hline \end{array}$$

5.
$$\begin{array}{r} 117.7 \\ + 96.037 \\ \hline \end{array}$$

6.
$$\begin{array}{r} 14.5933 \\ .6 \\ + 1.01 \\ \hline \end{array}$$

7.
$$\begin{array}{r} 49.3211 \\ 7.19 \\ + 3. \\ \hline \end{array}$$

8.
$$\begin{array}{r} .4499 \\ 3.3 \\ + 12.0729 \\ \hline \end{array}$$

9.
$$\begin{array}{r} 5.0555 \\ 137.05 \\ + 1.1 \\ \hline \end{array}$$

10.
$$\begin{array}{r} 10. \\ .6 \\ + 3.999 \\ \hline \end{array}$$

11.
$$4 + 10.6 + .325 =$$
$$\begin{array}{r} 4.000 \\ 10.600 \\ + .325 \\ \hline 14.925 \end{array}$$

12.
$$785.09 + 1 + .5 =$$

13.
$$12.01 + 6 + 3.7 =$$

14.
$$19.0445 + 23 + .889 =$$

15.
$$34.6789 + 545.338 + 2.5678 =$$

Application

Macy is buying school supplies. She is rounding to the nearest dollar the price of each item she buys so that she can stay within her budget.

Example Macy wants to buy a box of pencils for $1.19 and a package of paper for $1.69. About how much money will she need?

$1.19 rounds to $1.00 $1.00
$1.69 rounds to $2.00   + 2.00
                               $3.00

Macy will need about $3.00.

Solve.

1. Macy wants to buy a pen for $2.78 and a notebook for $.89. About how much money will she need?

   Answer_____

2. Macy stopped at the lunch counter. She bought a sandwich for $1.79 and a drink for $.75. About how much money did she spend for lunch?

   Answer_____

3. Macy wants to buy a backpack for $10.25 and a watch for $19.95. About how much money will she need?

   Answer_____

4. Macy wants to buy a paperback dictionary for $6.95 and a calculator for $7.59. About how much money will she need?

   Answer_____

Mixed Review

Change each fraction to a decimal.

1.
$$\frac{5}{10} =$$

2.
$$\frac{16}{100} =$$

3.
$$\frac{5}{20} =$$

4.
$$\frac{7}{25} =$$

5. twelve hundredths =

6. four fifths =

Add. Rename if necessary.

7. $7.50 + $3.50 =

8. $56.20 + $21.10 =

9. $109.26 + $96.04 =

10. $ .10 + $3.01 + $6.17 =

11. $11.26 + $ .98 + $102.06 =

12. $4 + $6.90 =

13. $6 + $15.89 =

14. $110 + $81.29 =

15.
```
  5.09
+ 6.3
```

16.
```
  7.12
+ 9.34
```

17.
```
  18.04
+ 25.7
```

18.
```
  .13
+ 2.09
```

19.
```
  2.0113
+ 7.5
```

20.
```
  .093
  .6
+ 25.07
```

21.
```
  50.139
  1.82
+   .011
```

22.
```
   .301
  115.12
+ 320.909
```

23.
```
  273.01
  134.131
+   6.81
```

24.
```
  497.263
  50.001
+ 148.294
```

25. 6.3 + 4.7 =

26. 8 + 76.2 + .18 =

27. 58 + 101.29 + 2.7 =

Subtracting Money

To subtract money, first line up the decimal points. Then subtract.
Rename if necessary. Remember to put a dollar sign in the answer and
to line up the decimal point in the answer with those in the problem.

$$\$5.96 - \$3.48 \qquad \begin{array}{r} {\scriptstyle 8\ 16} \\ \$5.\cancel{9}\cancel{6} \\ -\ \ 3.48 \\ \hline \$2.48 \end{array}$$

Use These Steps

Subtract $9.40 − $5.49

1. Set up the problem by lining up the decimal
   points.

$$\begin{array}{r} \$9.40 \\ -\ 5.49 \\ \hline \end{array}$$

2. Subtract. Begin with the digits on the right.
   Rename. Put a decimal point and a dollar
   sign in the answer.

$$\begin{array}{r} {\scriptstyle 13} \\ {\scriptstyle 8\ \cancel{3}\ 10} \\ \$\cancel{9}.\cancel{4}\,\cancel{0} \\ -\ 5.4\ 9 \\ \hline \$3.9\ 1 \end{array}$$

Subtract. Rename if necessary.

1.
$4.29 − $2.18 =

$$\begin{array}{r} \$4.29 \\ -\ 2.18 \\ \hline \$2.11 \end{array}$$

2. $8.88 − $ .52 =

3. $5.88 − $4.12 =

4.
$9.01 − $3.14 =

$$\begin{array}{r} {\scriptstyle 9} \\ {\scriptstyle 8\ \cancel{10}\ 11} \\ \$\cancel{9}.\cancel{0}\,\cancel{1} \\ -\ 3.1\ 4 \\ \hline \$5.8\ 7 \end{array}$$

5. $ .62 − $ .26 =

6. $8.46 − $ .98 =

7. $5.39 − $2.03 =

8. $8.77 − $ .93 =

9. $9.06 − $7.96 =

10. $7.20 − $2.75 =

11. $10.02 − $4.99 =

12. $1.03 − $ .56 =

Subtracting Money

When subtracting from a whole dollar amount, be sure to add a decimal point and two zeros. Rename if necessary.

$$
\begin{array}{r}
9 \\
4\,\cancel{10}\,10 \\
\$15 - \$3.97 \quad \$1\,\cancel{5}.\cancel{0}\,\cancel{0} \quad \longleftarrow \text{ add a decimal point and two zeros} \\
-\quad 3.9\,7 \\
\hline
\$1\,1.0\,3
\end{array}
$$

Use These Steps

Subtract $13 − $ .67

1. Set up the problem by lining up the decimal points. Add a decimal point and zeros.

$13.00 ◄— add a decimal point and two zeros
−   .67

2. Subtract. Begin with the digits on the right. Rename. Put a decimal point and a dollar sign in the answer.

$$
\begin{array}{r}
9 \\
2\,\cancel{10}\,10 \\
\$1\,\cancel{3}.\cancel{0}\,\cancel{0} \\
-\quad .6\,7 \\
\hline
\$1\,2.3\,3
\end{array}
$$

Subtract. Rename if necessary.

1.
$20 − $5.67 =

$$
\begin{array}{r}
9\ \ 9 \\
1\,\cancel{10}\,\cancel{10}\,10 \\
\$2\,\cancel{0}.\cancel{0}\,\cancel{0} \\
-\quad 5.6\,7 \\
\hline
\$1\,4.3\,3
\end{array}
$$

2.
$38 − $6.13 =

3.
$120 − $ .99 =

4.
$106 − $39.55 =

5.
$382 − $134.01 =

6.
$486 − $277.66 =

7.
$300 − $149.95 =

8.
$1,000 − $962.58 =

9.
$4,000 − $247.50 =

10. Sean had $20. He bought a magazine for $1.50. How much money does he have left?

11. Jules paid $10.75 for a CD. He gave the cashier $15. How much change did Jules get?

Answer_____

Answer_____

Subtracting Decimals

To subtract decimals, first set up the problem by lining up the decimal points just as with money.

Add a decimal point and zeros if needed so that both decimals have the same number of places after the decimal point. Then subtract. Line up the decimal point in the answer with the other decimal points. Rename if necessary.

$$10 - 9.3 \qquad \begin{array}{r} \overset{9}{\cancel{0}} \overset{10}{\cancel{10}} \, 10 \\ 1\,\cancel{0}.\cancel{0} \\ -\ 9.3 \\ \hline .7 \end{array} \leftarrow \text{add a decimal point and a zero}$$

Use These Steps

Subtract 14.06 − 1.325

1. Set up the problem by lining up the decimal points. Add a zero.

$$\begin{array}{r} 14.060 \leftarrow \text{add a zero} \\ -\ 1.325 \\ \hline \end{array}$$

2. Subtract. Begin with the digits on the right. Rename. Put a decimal point in the answer.

$$\begin{array}{r} {\scriptstyle 3\ 10\ 5\ 10} \\ 1\,4.0\,6\,0 \\ -\ 1.3\,2\,5 \\ \hline 1\,2.7\,3\,5 \end{array}$$

Subtract. Rename if necessary.

1.
$$\begin{array}{r} {\scriptstyle 8\ 10} \\ 3.9\cancel{0} \\ -\ 2.63 \\ \hline 1.27 \end{array}$$

2.
$$\begin{array}{r} 8.3 \\ -\ 5.21 \\ \hline \end{array}$$

3.
$$\begin{array}{r} 2. \\ -\ 1.01 \\ \hline \end{array}$$

4.
$$\begin{array}{r} .1 \\ -\ .09 \\ \hline \end{array}$$

5.
$$\begin{array}{r} 1. \\ -\ .13 \\ \hline \end{array}$$

6.
$$\begin{array}{r} 16.3 \\ -\ 2.81 \\ \hline \end{array}$$

7.
$$\begin{array}{r} 9. \\ -\ .3 \\ \hline \end{array}$$

8.
$$\begin{array}{r} 4. \\ -\ 3.42 \\ \hline \end{array}$$

9.
$$\begin{array}{r} 9.04 \\ -\ 1.035 \\ \hline \end{array}$$

10.
$$\begin{array}{r} .72 \\ -\ .349 \\ \hline \end{array}$$

11. $8.26 - 4.6 =$

12. $3.002 - .01 =$

13. $8 - 5.09 =$

14. $1 - .873 =$

15. $9.3 - 3.44 =$

16. $1 - .044 =$

17. $2.01 - 1.024 =$

18. $4 - .241 =$

19. $.6 - .455 =$

20. $.78 - .194 =$

Subtracting Decimals

When subtracting decimals, be sure to line up the decimal points. Add a
decimal point and zeros when needed. Rename if necessary.

$$1003 - 956.473$$

$$
\begin{array}{r}
\overset{9\ 9\,12\,9\ 9}{1\ 0\ 0\ 3.0\ 0\ 0} \leftarrow \text{add a decimal point and three zeroes} \\
-\ \ 9\ 5\ 6.4\ 7\ 3 \\
\hline
4\ 6.5\ 2\ 7
\end{array}
$$

Use These Steps

Subtract 275.5 − 198.75

1. Set up the problem by lining up the decimal points. Add a zero.

$$
\begin{array}{r}
275.50 \leftarrow \text{add a zero} \\
-\ 198.75
\end{array}
$$

2. Subtract. Begin with the digits on the right. Rename. Put a decimal point in the answer.

$$
\begin{array}{r}
\overset{16\,14\,14}{\overset{1\ 6\ 4\ 4\ 10}{2\ 7\ 5.5\ 0}} \\
-\ 1\ 9\ 8.7\ 5 \\
\hline
7\ 6.7\ 5
\end{array}
$$

Subtract. Rename if necessary.

1.
$$
\begin{array}{r}
\overset{12}{\overset{7\ 2\ 10}{.8\ 3\ 0}} \\
-\ .1\ 3\ 1 \\
\hline
.6\ 9\ 9
\end{array}
$$

2.
$$
\begin{array}{r}
8.612 \\
-\ 1.44
\end{array}
$$

3.
$$
\begin{array}{r}
20. \\
-\ 8.17
\end{array}
$$

4.
$$
\begin{array}{r}
86.21 \\
-\ .3
\end{array}
$$

5.
$$
\begin{array}{r}
115.1 \\
-\ 27.89
\end{array}
$$

6.
$$
\begin{array}{r}
82. \\
-\ 3.67
\end{array}
$$

7.
$$
\begin{array}{r}
103.1 \\
-\ 17.12
\end{array}
$$

8.
$$
\begin{array}{r}
93.28 \\
-\ .391
\end{array}
$$

9.
$$
\begin{array}{r}
931.001 \\
-\ 50.01
\end{array}
$$

10.
$$
\begin{array}{r}
810.0 \\
-\ 23.77
\end{array}
$$

11. $8 - 7.26 =$

12. $36.4 - .59 =$

13. $300 - 1.031 =$

14. $2 - .006 =$

15. Tony spends 40 hours a month studying. So far he has studied 27.5 hours. How many more hours does he need to study?

16. Tony practices his horn 8 hours a week. If he has practiced 6.29 hours so far today, how many more hours does he have to practice?

Answer_____

Answer_____

Problem Solving: Using a Table

The table below shows the income of people based on how many years of school they've completed. For example, of those people who have an elementary education, 4,945 thousand have an income of less than $10,000 a year.

AMOUNT OF EDUCATION (Numbers in thousands)	INCOME LEVEL					
	Under $10,000	$10,000–$14,999	$15,000–$24,999	$25,000–$34,999	$35,000–$49,999	$50,000 and over
Elementary	4,945	1,978	2,265.5	1,138.5	736	425.5
High School	7,879.1	4,924.4	8,946	7,304.6	6,976.3	5,047.6
College (one or more years)	2,297.8	1,931.5	5,028.5	5,428.1	7,559.3	11,122.5

Example What is the total number of people who have a high school education and receive an income of $25,000 or more a year?

Step 1. Find the row that shows the numbers of people with a high school education.

Step 2. Add the number of people with a high school education in the columns $25,000–$34,999, $35,000–$49,999, and $50,000 and over to find the total number of people receiving an income of $25,000 or more.

$$
\begin{array}{r}
1\ 1\ 1\ 1\\
7{,}304.6\\
6{,}976.3\\
+\ 5{,}047.6\\
\hline
19{,}328.5
\end{array}
$$

19,328.5 thousand people with a high school education have an income of $25,000 or more a year.

Solve.

1. What is the total number of people with an elementary education who earn $25,000 or more a year?

2. What is the total number of people with one or more years of college who earn $25,000 or more a year?

Answer _____

Answer _____

3. How many more people with a high school education earn $15,000–$24,999 than earn under $10,000?

Answer_____

4. Which income column lists the greatest number of people with an elementary education?

Answer_____

5. Which income column lists the greatest number of people with a high school education?

Answer_____

6. What is the total number of people who earn less than $10,000 a year?

Answer_____

7. What is the total number of people who earn $50,000 and over a year?

Answer_____

8. What is the total number of people with an elementary education who earn $14,999 or less a year?

Answer_____

9. What is the total number of people with a high school education who earn $14,999 or less a year?

Answer_____

10. What is the total number of people with one or more years of college who earn $14,999 or less a year?

Answer_____

11. Which income column shows the greatest number of people with one or more years of college?

Answer_____

12. Do most people with an income of $25,000–$34,999 have an elementary education, high school education, or one or more years of college?

Answer_____

Unit 2 Review

Add. Rename if necessary.

1.
$8.26 + $3.18 =

2.
$30.40 + $24.77 =

3.
$120.34 + $18.25 =

4.
$ .25 + $3.50 + $8.75 =

5.
$103.25 + $98.09 + $201.60 =

6.
$5 + $7.70 =

7.
$8.25 + $11 =

8.
$103.36 + $180 =

9.
```
  6.39
+ 2.81
```

10.
```
  8.36
+ 5.2
```

11.
```
  30.18
+ 26.88
```

12.
```
  81.001
+   3.7
```

13.
```
  102.113
+  37.32
```

14.
```
   .83
   .29
+ 13.629
```

15.
```
  83.316
   2.1
+  9.699
```

16.
```
  263.101
   77.92
+  81.98
```

17.
```
   .312
  31.8
+ 729.299
```

18.
```
  426.813
   59.93
+ 186.399
```

19.
2.3 + .9 + .38 =

20.
10 + 81.7 + 8.7 =

21.
190 + 26.39 + 3.9 =

22.
.1556 + 32 + 1.9 =

23.
57.9921 + 543.02 + 6 =

24.
125.4 + .001 + .0378 =

Subtract. Rename if necessary.

25.
$8.26 − $3.13 =

26.
$13.74 − $4.54 =

27.
$23.11 − $16.12 =

28.
$121.81 − $76.15 =

29.
$183.12 − $28.06 =

30.
$118.59 − $94.63

31.
$6 − $1.89 =

32.
$410 − $339.31 =

33.
$28 − $12.38 =

34.
$$\begin{array}{r} 10.001 \\ -\ 5.31 \\ \hline \end{array}$$

35.
$$\begin{array}{r} 3.8 \\ -\ 1.95 \\ \hline \end{array}$$

36.
$$\begin{array}{r} 16.02 \\ -\ 9.9 \\ \hline \end{array}$$

37.
$$\begin{array}{r} 76.01 \\ -\ .133 \\ \hline \end{array}$$

38.
$$\begin{array}{r} 11.384 \\ -\ 9.499 \\ \hline \end{array}$$

39.
$$\begin{array}{r} 26.03 \\ -\ 18.3 \\ \hline \end{array}$$

40.
$$\begin{array}{r} 113.021 \\ -\ 1.139 \\ \hline \end{array}$$

41.
$$\begin{array}{r} 123.09 \\ -\ 99.1 \\ \hline \end{array}$$

42.
$$\begin{array}{r} 499. \\ -\ 28.991 \\ \hline \end{array}$$

43.
$$\begin{array}{r} 233.1 \\ -\ 129.61 \\ \hline \end{array}$$

44.
26.7 − 18.3 =

45.
101 − 76.23 =

46.
111.28 − 23.98 =

47.
50 − .0032 =

48.
6 − .093 =

49.
.073 − .06154 =

Below is a list of the problems in this review and the pages on which the skills are taught. If you missed any problems, turn to the pages listed and practice the skills. Then correct the problems you missed in the Unit Review.

Problems	Pages	Problems	Pages
1-5	33	25-30	39
6-8	34	31-33	40
9-24	35-36	34-49	41-42

You can multiply and divide decimals to figure out your gas mileage, your total costs, or your proceeds from a fundraiser.

Multiplying and dividing decimals is done the same way as multiplying and dividing whole numbers. You must be careful, however, to put decimal points in the correct place in the answers.

Getting Ready

You should be familiar with the skills on this page and the next before you begin this unit.

 When you are working with decimals, place value is important in setting up problems, renaming, and lining up answers.

Write the value of the underlined digit in each number.

1.
1.2̲4   2 tenths
_____

2.
.07̲9
_____

3.
42.93̲
_____

4.
5.506̲
_____

5.
346.828̲5
_____

6.
.001̲3
_____

Getting Ready

When setting up problems for multiplication, be sure to line up the digits in the correct columns.

Multiply.

7.

$32 \times 5 =$

$$\begin{array}{r} 1 \\ 32 \\ \times\ \ 5 \\ \hline 160 \end{array}$$

8.

$406 \times 28 =$

9.

$1{,}029 \times 87 =$

10.

$2{,}188 \times 346 =$

For review, see pages 89–92, 95–98, 105–113 in **Math Skills for Life, Whole Numbers.**

When setting up problems for division, be sure to put the number you are dividing by in front of the $\big)$.

Divide. Write remainders as fractions in lowest terms.

11.

$44 \div 6 =$

$$\begin{array}{r} 7\ \frac{2}{6} = 7\frac{1}{3} \\ 6\overline{)44} \\ -\ 42 \\ \hline 2 \end{array}$$

12.

$800 \div 31 =$

13.

$2{,}403 \div 24 =$

14.

$6{,}498 \div 722 =$

For review, see pages 130–131, 134–137, 140–142, 147–148 in **Math Skills for Life, Whole Numbers.**

When multiplying and dividing decimals, you may need to round your answers.

Round to the nearest whole number.

15.

$1.45 = 1$

16.

$.521 =$

17.

$17.9 =$

18.

$10.04 =$

19.

$.06 =$

Round to the nearest tenth.

20.

$2.09 = 2.1$

21.

$5.77 =$

22.

$20.241 =$

23.

$.953 =$

24.

$45.81 =$

Round to the nearest hundredth.

25.

$5.033 = 5.03$

26.

$.489 =$

27.

$1.001 =$

28.

$14.615 =$

29.

$200.0004 =$

For review, see Unit 1, pages 25–27.

Multiplying Money

When you multiply money by a whole number, first set up the problem by lining up the digits starting at the right. Place the decimal point in your answer so that there are two places to the right of the decimal point. Include a dollar sign in the answer.

$$\$6.25 \times 3 = \quad \begin{array}{r} 1 \\ \$6.25 \\ \times \quad 3 \\ \hline \$18.75 \end{array} \leftarrow \text{two decimal places}$$

18 dollars and 75 cents

Use These Steps

Multiply $4.31 × 4

1. Set up the problem.

$$\begin{array}{r} \$4.31 \\ \times \quad 4 \\ \hline \end{array}$$

2. Multiply. Rename.

$$\begin{array}{r} 1 \\ \$4.31 \\ \times \quad 4 \\ \hline 17\ 24 \end{array}$$

3. Put a decimal point and a dollar sign in the answer.

$$\begin{array}{r} 1 \\ \$4.31 \\ \times \quad 4 \\ \hline \$17.24 \end{array} \leftarrow \text{two decimal places}$$

Multiply.

1.

$2.97 \times 5 =$

$$\begin{array}{r} 4\ 3 \\ \$2.97 \\ \times \quad 5 \\ \hline \$14.85 \end{array}$$

2.

$9.49 \times 6 =$

3.

$3.26 \times 9 =$

4.

$7.85 \times 8 =$

5.

$$\begin{array}{r} \$1.99 \\ \times \quad 7 \\ \hline \end{array}$$

6.

$$\begin{array}{r} \$6.25 \\ \times \quad 4 \\ \hline \end{array}$$

7.

$$\begin{array}{r} \$8.03 \\ \times \quad 6 \\ \hline \end{array}$$

8.

$$\begin{array}{r} \$9.60 \\ \times \quad 5 \\ \hline \end{array}$$

9.

$ .57 \times 9 =$

$$\begin{array}{r} 6 \\ \$ .57 \\ \times \quad 9 \\ \hline \$5.13 \end{array}$$

10.

$ .08 \times 2 =$

11.

$ .30 \times 7 =$

12.

$ .99 \times 3 =$

Multiplying Money

You multiply larger amounts of money the same way you multiply smaller amounts. Be sure to include a decimal point and dollar sign in the answer.

Use These Steps

Multiply $10.92 × 11

1. Set up the problem.

$$\begin{array}{r} \$10.92 \\ \times\ \ \ \ 11 \end{array}$$

2. Multiply.

$$\begin{array}{r} \$10.92 \\ \times\ \ \ \ 11 \\ \hline 1092 \\ +\ 1092 \\ \hline 12012 \end{array}$$

3. Put a decimal point and dollar sign in the answer.

$$\begin{array}{r} \$\ 10.92 \\ \times\ \ \ \ 11 \\ \hline 10\ 92 \\ +\ 109\ 2 \\ \hline \$120.12 \end{array}$$ ◄—— two decimal places

Multiply.

1.

$9.52 × 25 =

$$\begin{array}{r} \$9.52 \\ \times\ \ \ \ 25 \\ \hline 47\ 60 \\ +\ \ 190\ 4 \\ \hline \$238.00 \end{array}$$

2.

$13.79 × 32 =

3.

$25.39 × 19 =

4.

$49.97 × 12 =

5.

$$\begin{array}{r} \$79.38 \\ \times\ \ \ \ 24 \end{array}$$

6.

$$\begin{array}{r} \$102.45 \\ \times\ \ \ \ 52 \end{array}$$

7.

$$\begin{array}{r} \$98.93 \\ \times\ \ \ \ 17 \end{array}$$

8.

$$\begin{array}{r} \$306.25 \\ \times\ \ \ \ 44 \end{array}$$

9. Ms. Adams pays $325.50 for rent each month. How much rent does she pay a year?
(Hint: 1 year = 12 months)

Answer_____

10. Mrs. Zuniga pays $143.27 on a loan each month. If she pays this amount for 48 months, how much will she pay in all?

Answer_____

Multiplying Money by 10, 100, and 1,000

When you multiply by 10, 100, or 1,000, you don't have to write a row of partial products with zeros. There is an easier way to multiply amounts of money by 10, 100, or 1,000.

Use These Steps

Multiply $9.98 × 100

1. Since there are two zeros in 100, add two zeros to $9.98.

    $9.98 × 100 = $9.98<u>00</u>

2. Move the decimal point two places to the right. Be sure a dollar sign is in the answer.

    $9.9800 = $998.00

Multiply.

1.
$ .49 × 10 = $4.90

2.
$ .25 × 10 =

3.
$ .90 × 10 =

4.
$2.31 × 10 =

5.
$3.90 × 10 =

6.
$58.06 × 10 =

7.
$5.57 × 100 = $557.00

8.
$13.20 × 100 =

9.
$76.09 × 100 =

10.
$240.65 × 100 =

11.
$653.30 × 100 =

12.
$500.03 × 100 =

13.
$7.92 × 1,000 = $7,920.00

14.
$1.40 × 1,000 =

15.
$4.06 × 1,000 =

16.
$25.29 × 1,000 =

17.
$80.30 × 1,000 =

18.
$320.07 × 1,000 =

19.
$412.27 × 10 =

20.
$ .67 × 100 =

21.
$37.04 × 1,000 =

Multiplying Decimals by Whole Numbers

To multiply other decimals by whole numbers, be sure to line up the digits the same way you do with amounts of money. The decimal point in the answer needs to show the total number of decimal places to the right of the decimal point in the problem.

$$4.2 \times 3 = \qquad \begin{array}{r} 4.2 \\ \times 3 \\ \hline 12.6 \end{array}$$

4.2 ◄— one decimal place
× 3 ◄— no decimal places
12.6 ◄— one decimal place

Use These Steps

Multiply 9.62 × 5

1. Set up the problem.

$$\begin{array}{r} 9.62 \\ \times 5 \\ \hline \end{array}$$

2. Multiply. Rename.

$$\begin{array}{r} \scriptstyle 3\,1 \\ 9.62 \\ \times 5 \\ \hline 4810 \end{array}$$

3. Put a decimal point in the answer.

$$\begin{array}{r} \scriptstyle 3\,1 \\ 9.62 \\ \times 5 \\ \hline 48.10 \end{array}$$

9.62 ◄— two decimal places
× 5 ◄— no decimal places
48.10 ◄— two decimal places

Multiply.

1.
$3.6 \times 9 =$

$$\begin{array}{r} \scriptstyle 5 \\ 3.6 \\ \times 9 \\ \hline 32.4 \end{array}$$

2.
$.5 \times 4 =$

3.
$7.2 \times 8 =$

4.
$16.4 \times 7 =$

5.
$.32 \times 5 =$

$$\begin{array}{r} \scriptstyle 1 \\ .32 \\ \times 5 \\ \hline 1.60 \end{array}$$

6.
$10.51 \times 6 =$

7.
$.08 \times 3 =$

8.
$2.78 \times 9 =$

9.
$$\begin{array}{r} 7.3 \\ \times 4 \\ \hline \end{array}$$

10.
$$\begin{array}{r} .06 \\ \times 7 \\ \hline \end{array}$$

11.
$$\begin{array}{r} .7 \\ \times 5 \\ \hline \end{array}$$

12.
$$\begin{array}{r} 30.29 \\ \times 2 \\ \hline \end{array}$$

13.
$$\begin{array}{r} 51.02 \\ \times 6 \\ \hline \end{array}$$

14.
$$\begin{array}{r} 34.8 \\ \times 2 \\ \hline \end{array}$$

15.
$$\begin{array}{r} .45 \\ \times 4 \\ \hline \end{array}$$

16.
$$\begin{array}{r} 10.01 \\ \times 3 \\ \hline \end{array}$$

Multiplying Decimals by Whole Numbers

Count the places to the right of the decimal point in the problem. Be sure the decimal point in the answer shows the total number of decimal places to the right of the decimal point in the problem.

Use These Steps

Multiply 5.039 × 17

1. Set up the problem.

$$\begin{array}{r} 5.039 \\ \times\ \ \ 17 \end{array}$$

2. Multiply. Rename.

$$\begin{array}{r} 26\ \ \ \ \ \ \\ 5.039 \\ \times\ \ \ 17 \\ \hline 35273 \\ +\ 5039\ \ \\ \hline 85663 \end{array}$$

3. Put a decimal point in the answer.

$$\begin{array}{r} 26\ \ \ \ \ \ \\ 5.039 \\ \times\ \ \ 17 \\ \hline 35\ 273 \\ +\ 50\ 39\ \ \\ \hline 85.663 \end{array}$$

5.039 ← three decimal places
17 ← no decimal places
85.663 ← three decimal places

Multiply.

1.
$2.341 \times 25 =$

$$\begin{array}{r} 2.341 \\ \times\ \ \ 25 \\ \hline 11\ 705 \\ +\ 46\ 82\ \ \\ \hline 58.525 \end{array}$$

2.
$.053 \times 31 =$

3.
$28.027 \times 46 =$

4.
$39.005 \times 53 =$

5.
$6.218 \times 182 =$

6.
$.509 \times 246 =$

7.
$12.098 \times 425 =$

8.
$37.186 \times 931 =$

9. In one state you pay $.085 in sales tax for each dollar you spend. If you spend $14, how much tax will you pay? Round the answer to the nearest hundredth, or cent.
(Hint: Multiply the tax rate by the amount of the purchase.)

10. The sales tax rate in another state is $.065. If you spend $120, how much will the tax be? Round the answer to the nearest hundredth, or cent.

Answer_____

Answer_____

Multiplying Decimals by 10, 100, and 1,000

To multiply a decimal by 10, 100, or 1,000, move the decimal point to the right the same number of places as there are zeros in the number you are multiplying by. You may need to add one or more zeros to get the correct number of places.

$2.4 \times 10 = 2.4 = 24$ $2.4 \times 100 = 2.40 = 240$ $2.4 \times 1,000 = 2.400 = 2,400$

Use These Steps

Multiply .913 × 100

1. **Count how many zeros there are in 100.**

   There are two.

2. **Move the decimal point two places to the right.**

   $.913 \times 100 = .913 = 91.3$

Multiply.

1. $.5 \times 10 = 5$

2. $3.2 \times 10 =$

3. $15.6 \times 10 =$

4. $132.9 \times 10 =$

5. $6.17 \times 10 = 61.7$

6. $.98 \times 10 =$

7. $72.36 \times 10 =$

8. $241.05 \times 10 =$

9. $1.3 \times 100 = 130$

10. $.5 \times 100 =$

11. $8.6 \times 100 =$

12. $510.7 \times 100 =$

13. $4.67 \times 100 =$

14. $1.58 \times 100 =$

15. $.98 \times 100 =$

16. $423.02 \times 100 =$

17. $.5 \times 1,000 = 500$

18. $19.3 \times 1,000 =$

19. $5.7 \times 1,000 =$

20. $115.2 \times 1,000 =$

21. $.32 \times 1,000 =$

22. $8.51 \times 1,000 =$

23. $1.07 \times 1,000 =$

24. $266.29 \times 1,000 =$

25. $.865 \times 10 =$

26. $1.207 \times 100 =$

27. $10.036 \times 1,000 =$

28. $372.331 \times 10 =$

29. $7.314 \times 1,000 =$

30. $.802 \times 10 =$

31. $11.006 \times 1,000 =$

32. $659.078 \times 100 =$

Multiplying Decimals by Decimals

To multiply a decimal by another decimal, first multiply the way you do whole numbers. Then count the number of decimal places in the problem. Put a decimal point in the answer to show the total number of decimal places you counted. Always count from the right.

$$
\begin{array}{r}
10.39 \leftarrow \text{two decimal places} \\
\times\ \ .06 \leftarrow \text{two decimal places} \\
\hline
.6234 \leftarrow \text{four decimal places}
\end{array}
$$

Use These Steps

Multiply 3.247 × 1.5

1. Set up the problem.

$$
\begin{array}{r}
3.247 \\
\times\ \ 1.5 \\
\end{array}
$$

2. Multiply. Rename.

$$
\begin{array}{r}
1\ 2\ 3 \\
3.247 \\
\times\ \ \ 1.5 \\
\hline
16235 \\
+\ 3247 \\
\hline
48705
\end{array}
$$

3. Put a decimal point in the answer.

$$
\begin{array}{r}
1\ 2\ 3 \\
3.247 \leftarrow \text{three decimal places} \\
\times\ \ \ 1.5 \leftarrow \text{one decimal place} \\
\hline
1\ 6235 \\
+\ 3\ 247 \\
\hline
4.8705 \leftarrow \text{four decimal places}
\end{array}
$$

Multiply.

1.

$5.6 \times 1.8 =$

$$
\begin{array}{r}
4 \\
5.6 \\
\times 1.8 \\
\hline
4\ 4\ 8 \\
+5\ 6 \\
\hline
10.0\ 8
\end{array}
$$

2.

$9.04 \times 3.2 =$

3.

$.99 \times .5 =$

4.

$.3 \times .7 =$

5.

$15.3 \times 3.12 =$

6.

$8.29 \times 4.33 =$

7.

$7.851 \times .03 =$

8.

$25.2 \times .75 =$

9.

$$
\begin{array}{r}
82.9 \\
\times\ 2.6 \\
\end{array}
$$

10.

$$
\begin{array}{r}
60.08 \\
\times\ \ .07 \\
\end{array}
$$

11.

$$
\begin{array}{r}
9.272 \\
\times\ 5.01 \\
\end{array}
$$

12.

$$
\begin{array}{r}
75.2 \\
\times\ 3.29 \\
\end{array}
$$

Multiplying Decimals by Decimals

Sometimes the answer does not have enough digits to show the correct number of decimal places. When this happens, you need to insert one or more zeros between the answer and the decimal point. The zeros serve as place holders so you can show the correct number of places.

$$.185 \leftarrow \text{three decimal places}$$
$$\underline{\times \ \ .12} \leftarrow \text{two decimal places}$$
$$370$$
$$\underline{+ \ \ 185}$$
$$.02220 \leftarrow \text{five decimal places}$$
$$\overbrace{\qquad} \text{insert a zero}$$

Use These Steps

Multiply .4 × .1

1. Set up the problem.

$$.4$$
$$\underline{\times .1}$$

2. Multiply.

$$.4$$
$$\underline{\times .1}$$
$$4$$

3. Insert a zero. Put a decimal point in the answer.

$$.4 \leftarrow \text{one decimal place}$$
$$\underline{\times .1} \leftarrow \text{one decimal place}$$
$$.04 \leftarrow \text{two decimal places}$$
$$\uparrow \text{insert a zero}$$

Multiply.

1.
.3 × .2 =
$$.3$$
$$\underline{\times .2}$$
$$.06$$

2.
.4 × .2 =

3.
.16 × .12 =

4.
.09 × .06 =

5.
41.3 × .001 =

6.
.303 × .22 =

7.
1.31 × .021 =

8.
.095 × .067 =

9.
5.15 × .3 =

10.
6.4 × .104 =

11.
9.08 × .13 =

12.
70.1 × .04 =

Application

You multiply decimals to find the total cost when you know the price per unit.

Example Honey costs $3.82 cents a pound. How much does five pounds cost?

```
      4 1
   $3.82
 ×     5
  $19.10
```

Five pounds of honey costs $19.10.

Solve. Round the answers to the nearest hundredth, or cent.

1. Apples cost $ .69 a pound. How much do 10 pounds cost?

    Answer_____

2. Eggs cost $ .89 a dozen. How much do 3 dozen cost?

    Answer_____

3. Swordfish costs $13.00 a pound. How much does .5 pound cost?

    Answer_____

4. Granola costs $2.99 a pound. How much does 1.5 pounds cost?

    Answer_____

5. Fancy coffee beans cost $5.75 a pound. How much do 2.35 pounds cost?

    Answer_____

6. One pound of butter costs $1.69. How much does .25 pound cost?

    Answer_____

Mixed Review

Add, subtract, or multiply.

1.
$$
\begin{array}{r}
\$3.95 \\
+\ \ .32 \\
\hline
\end{array}
$$

2.
$$
\begin{array}{r}
\$1.39 \\
-\ \ .79 \\
\hline
\end{array}
$$

3.
$$
\begin{array}{r}
\$2.29 \\
\times\ \ \ \ 6 \\
\hline
\end{array}
$$

4.
$$
\begin{array}{r}
\$5.00 \\
-\ 4.37 \\
\hline
\end{array}
$$

5.
$$
\begin{array}{r}
\$10.98 \\
+\ \ 3.65 \\
\hline
\end{array}
$$

6.
$$
\begin{array}{r}
\$\ .59 \\
\times\ \ \ 12 \\
\hline
\end{array}
$$

7.
$$
\begin{array}{r}
\$36.00 \\
-\ \ \ 9.23 \\
\hline
\end{array}
$$

8.
$$
\begin{array}{r}
\$8.99 \\
\times\ \ \ 10 \\
\hline
\end{array}
$$

9.
$$
\begin{array}{r}
\$\ .25 \\
+\ \ .75 \\
\hline
\end{array}
$$

10.
$$
\begin{array}{r}
\$12.05 \\
-\ \ \ 6.92 \\
\hline
\end{array}
$$

11.
$$
\begin{array}{r}
.47 \\
+.93 \\
\hline
\end{array}
$$

12.
$$
\begin{array}{r}
2.05 \\
-\ .79 \\
\hline
\end{array}
$$

13.
$$
\begin{array}{r}
31.3 \\
\times\ \ 4.9 \\
\hline
\end{array}
$$

14.
$$
\begin{array}{r}
4. \\
+3.6 \\
\hline
\end{array}
$$

15.
$$
\begin{array}{r}
6.01 \\
-4.99 \\
\hline
\end{array}
$$

16.
$$
\begin{array}{r}
1.5 \\
-\ .7 \\
\hline
\end{array}
$$

17.
$$
\begin{array}{r}
14.06 \\
\times\ \ \ \ 20 \\
\hline
\end{array}
$$

18.
$$
\begin{array}{r}
6.23 \\
+\ .59 \\
\hline
\end{array}
$$

19.
$$
\begin{array}{r}
.4 \\
\times .2 \\
\hline
\end{array}
$$

20.
$$
\begin{array}{r}
25.3 \\
\times\ \ \ 8 \\
\hline
\end{array}
$$

21.
$$
\begin{array}{r}
.325 \\
+.987 \\
\hline
\end{array}
$$

22.
$$
\begin{array}{r}
7.022 \\
-1.853 \\
\hline
\end{array}
$$

23.
$$
\begin{array}{r}
10.344 \\
+\ 5.6 \\
\hline
\end{array}
$$

24.
$$
\begin{array}{r}
1.472 \\
\times\ \ \ \ 10 \\
\hline
\end{array}
$$

25.
$$
\begin{array}{r}
16.021 \\
\times\ \ \ \ .7 \\
\hline
\end{array}
$$

26.
$$
\begin{array}{r}
13.491 \\
+\ \ .281 \\
\hline
\end{array}
$$

27.
$$
\begin{array}{r}
532.065 \\
-\ 93.279 \\
\hline
\end{array}
$$

28.
$$
\begin{array}{r}
49.006 \\
\times\ \ \ \ .32 \\
\hline
\end{array}
$$

29.
$$
\begin{array}{r}
1.610 \\
-\ .234 \\
\hline
\end{array}
$$

30.
$$
\begin{array}{r}
.256 \\
\times\ .19 \\
\hline
\end{array}
$$

31.
$$
\begin{array}{r}
8.521 \\
\times\ \ \ 25 \\
\hline
\end{array}
$$

32.
$$
\begin{array}{r}
2.035 \\
-\ .216 \\
\hline
\end{array}
$$

33.
$$
\begin{array}{r}
154. \\
-\ 29.326 \\
\hline
\end{array}
$$

34.
$$
\begin{array}{r}
1.846 \\
\times\ \ .75 \\
\hline
\end{array}
$$

35.
$$
\begin{array}{r}
.051 \\
\times\ .09 \\
\hline
\end{array}
$$

Dividing Money

To divide amounts of money, first set up the problem. Put a decimal point in the answer above the decimal point in the problem. Put a dollar sign in the answer.

$$\$7.70 \div 5$$

$$
\begin{array}{r}
\$1.54 \\
5\overline{)\,\$7.70} \\
-5 \\
\hline
27 \\
-25 \\
\hline
20 \\
-20 \\
\hline
0
\end{array}
$$

Use These Steps

Divide $4.96 ÷ 8

1. Set up the problem.

$$8\overline{)\,\$4.96}$$

2. Put a dollar sign and a decimal point in the answer.

$$
\begin{array}{r}
\$\ . \\
8\overline{)\,\$4.96}
\end{array}
$$

3. Divide.

$$
\begin{array}{r}
\$\ .62 \\
8\overline{)\,\$4.96} \\
-48 \\
\hline
16 \\
-16 \\
\hline
0
\end{array}
$$

Divide.

1.

$$\$5.04 \div 6 =$$

$$
\begin{array}{r}
\$\ .84 \\
6\overline{)\,\$5.04} \\
-48 \\
\hline
24 \\
-24 \\
\hline
0
\end{array}
$$

2.

$$\$2.79 \div 9 =$$

3.

$$\$\ .36 \div 4 =$$

4.

$$\$1.00 \div 5 =$$

5.

$$\$9.84 \div 8 =$$

6.

$$\$12.60 \div 6 =$$

7.

$$\$17.37 \div 3 =$$

8.

$$\$62.86 \div 7 =$$

Dividing Money

Sometimes when you divide amounts of money, you have a remainder.
When this happens, divide to three decimal places. Then round to the
nearest hundredth. This is the same as rounding to the nearest cent.

Use These Steps

Divide $9.23 ÷ 16

1. Set up the problem. Put a
dollar sign and a decimal
point in the answer.

$$\begin{array}{r} \$ \\ 16\overline{)\$9.23} \end{array}$$

2. Add a zero so that you can
divide to three decimal
places.

$$\begin{array}{r} \$.576 \\ 16\overline{)\$9.230} \\ -8\,0 \\ \hline 1\,23 \\ -1\,12 \\ \hline 110 \\ -96 \\ \hline 14 \end{array}$$

3. Ignore the remainder.
Round the answer to the
nearest hundredth, or cent.

$.576 rounds to $ .58

Divide. Round each answer to the nearest hundredth, or cent.

1.
$13.40 ÷ 32 =

$$\begin{array}{r} \$.418 \\ 32\overline{)\$13.400} \\ -12\,8 \\ \hline 60 \\ -32 \\ \hline 280 \\ -256 \\ \hline 24 \end{array}$$

$ .418 rounds to $ .42

2.
$21.36 ÷ 15 =

3.
$427.00 ÷ 26 =

4.
$5.89 ÷ 11 =

5.
$$49\overline{)\$178.90}$$

6.
$$62\overline{)\$308.00}$$

7.
$$36\overline{)\$27.06}$$

8.
$$50\overline{)\$152.75}$$

Dividing Money by 10, 100, and 1,000

When you divide amounts of money by 10, 100, or 1,000, you don't have to set up the problem. Move the decimal point to the left the same number of places as there are zeros in the number you are dividing by. You may need to insert zeros as place holders between the answer and the decimal point.

Use These Steps

Divide $ .92 ÷ 10

1. Since there is one zero in 10, move the decimal point one place to the left.

$ .92 ÷ 10 = $ .92 = $ .092

insert a zero

2. Round to two decimal places.

$ .092 rounds to $ .09

Divide. Round to the nearest hundredth, or cent.

1.
$5.67 ÷ 10 = $ 5.67

$ .567 rounds to $ .57

2.
$ .40 ÷ 10 =

3.
$18.71 ÷ 10 =

4.
$4.01 ÷ 10 =

5.
$41.83 ÷ 10 =

6.
$ .78 ÷ 10 =

7.
$3.35 ÷ 100 = $ 3.35

$ .0335 rounds to $ .03

8.
$9.89 ÷ 100 =

9.
$10.06 ÷ 100 =

10.
$.65 ÷ 100 =

11.
$21.80 ÷ 100 =

12.
$127.35 ÷ 100 =

13.
$497.62 ÷ 1,000 = $ 497.62

$.49762 rounds to $.50

14.
$3,485.99 ÷ 1,000 =

15.
$700.00 ÷ 1,000 =

16.
$9.74 ÷ 1,000 =

17.
$35.75 ÷ 1,000 =

18.
$516.03 ÷ 1,000 =

19.
$30.77 ÷ 10 =

20.
$4.13 ÷ 100 =

21.
$16.50 ÷ 1,000 =

Dividing Decimals by Whole Numbers

To divide other decimals by whole numbers, set up the problem. Put a decimal point in the answer above the decimal point in the problem.

Use These Steps

Divide .408 ÷ 4

1. Set up the problem.

$$4\overline{).408}$$

2. Put a decimal point in the answer.

$$4\overline{).408}$$

3. Divide.

$$\begin{array}{r} .102 \\ 4\overline{).408} \\ -4 \\ \hline 00 \\ -0 \\ \hline 08 \\ -8 \\ \hline 0 \end{array}$$

Divide.

1.

$7.36 \div 8 =$

$$\begin{array}{r} .92 \\ 8\overline{)7.36} \\ -72 \\ \hline 16 \\ -16 \\ \hline 0 \end{array}$$

2. $5.2 \div 4 =$

3. $8.5 \div 5 =$

4. $.627 \div 3 =$

5. $.74 \div 2 =$

6. $123.6 \div 6 =$

7. $25.74 \div 9 =$

8. $.861 \div 7 =$

9. $10.2 \div 3 =$

10. $3.005 \div 5 =$

11. $1.68 \div 8 =$

12. $9.2 \div 4 =$

Dividing Decimals by Whole Numbers

Sometimes when dividing decimals, you get a remainder. When this happens, you can continue to divide by adding zeros to the number you are dividing into. Stop dividing when the remainder is zero, or when there are enough decimal places to round to a certain place. For example, to round to tenths, divide to two decimal places.

Use These Steps

Divide $17.3 \div 6$. **Round to the nearest tenth.**

1. Set up the problem. Put a decimal point in the answer.

$$6\overline{)17.3}$$

2. Add a zero so that you can divide to two decimal places.

$$\begin{array}{r} 2.88 \\ 6\overline{)17.30} \\ -12 \\ \hline 53 \\ -48 \\ \hline 50 \\ -48 \\ \hline 2 \end{array}$$

3. Round to the nearest tenth.

2.88 rounds to 2.9

Divide. Round to the nearest tenth.

1.

$20.3 \div 3 =$

$$\begin{array}{r} 6.76 \\ 3\overline{)20.30} \\ -18 \\ \hline 23 \\ -21 \\ \hline 20 \\ -18 \\ \hline 2 \end{array}$$

6.7 rounds to 6.8

2.

$76.41 \div 8 =$

3.

$100.0 \div 7 =$

4.

$9.7 \div 9 =$

Divide. Round to the nearest hundredth.

5.

$1.2 \div 25 =$

$$\begin{array}{r} .048 \\ 25\overline{)1.200} \\ -1\,00 \\ \hline 200 \\ -200 \\ \hline 0 \end{array}$$

.048 rounds to .05

6.

$1,480.29 \div 37 =$

7.

$5.281 \div 40 =$

8.

$.99 \div 15 =$

Dividing Decimals by 10, 100, and 1,000

When you divide by 10, 100, or 1,000, move the decimal point in the answer to the left the same number of places as there are zeros in the number you are dividing by.

Use These Steps

Divide 1.4 ÷ 100

1. There are two zeros in 100.

100

2. Move the decimal point two places to the left. Insert a zero.

1.4 ÷ 100 = 1.4 = .014

└──insert a zero

Divide.

1. .3 ÷ 10 = .03

2. 5.4 ÷ 10 =

3. 22.7 ÷ 10 =

4. .72 ÷ 10 =

5. 45.36 ÷ 10 =

6. 298.54 ÷ 10 =

7. 4.5 ÷ 100 = .045

8. .2 ÷ 100 =

9. 11.6 ÷ 100 =

10. .86 ÷ 100 =

11. 3.09 ÷ 100 =

12. 247.41 ÷ 100 =

13. 92.3 ÷ 1,000 = .0923

14. .4 ÷ 1,000 =

15. 311.6 ÷ 1,000 =

16. .47 ÷ 1,000 =

17. 3.21 ÷ 1,000 =

18. 86.55 ÷ 1,000 =

19. 1.802 ÷ 100 =

20. 29.004 ÷ 1,000 =

21. .407 ÷ 10 =

22. 100.255 ÷ 1,000 =

23. .573 ÷ 10 =

24. 6.102 ÷ 100 =

25. 39.027 ÷ 100 =

26. 766.341 ÷ 10 =

27. 4.011 ÷ 1,000 =

28. 75.403 ÷ 100 =

29. .886 ÷ 10 =

30. 137.429 ÷ 100 =

Dividing Whole Numbers by Decimals

To divide a whole number by a decimal, first move the decimal point to the right to make a whole number. Then move the decimal point in the number you are dividing into the same number of places to the right. Add one zero for each place you moved the decimal point. Put the decimal point in the answer directly above the decimal point in the number you are dividing into.

$$36 \div 1.5$$

$$
\begin{array}{r}
24 \\
1.5\overline{)360} \\
-30 \\
\hline
60 \\
-60 \\
\hline
0
\end{array}
$$

Use These Steps

Divide 48 ÷ .24

1. Set up the problem.

$$.24\overline{)48}$$

2. Move both decimal points two places to the right. Add two zeros. Put a decimal point in the answer.

$$.24\overline{)48.00}$$

3. Divide.

$$
\begin{array}{r}
200. \\
24\overline{)4800} \\
-48 \\
\hline
00 \\
-0 \\
\hline
00 \\
-0 \\
\hline
0
\end{array}
$$

Divide.

1.

$69 \div 2.3 =$

$$
\begin{array}{r}
30. \\
2.3\overline{)69.0} \\
-69 \\
\hline
00 \\
-0 \\
\hline
0
\end{array}
$$

2.

$42 \div 3.5 =$

3.

$993 \div .3 =$

4.

$124 \div .4 =$

5.

$580 \div 7.25 =$

6.

$165 \div .55 =$

7.

$806 \div 8.06 =$

8.

$278 \div 1.39 =$

Dividing Whole Numbers by Decimals

Sometimes when you divide whole numbers by decimals you get a remainder. When this happens, you can continue to divide by adding zeros to the number you are dividing into. Stop dividing when the remainder is zero, or when there are enough decimal places in the answer to round to a certain place.

Use These Steps

Divide 3 ÷ .8 Round to the nearest tenth.

1. Set up the problem.

$$.8\overline{)3}$$

2. Move both decimal points one place to the right. Add a zero. Put a decimal point in the answer.

$$.8\overline{)3.0}$$

3. Divide. Add zeros. Round to the nearest tenth.

```
      3.75
8)30.00
   -24
     60
    -56
      40
     -40
       0
```
3.75 rounds to 3.8

Divide. Round to the nearest tenth.

1.
6 ÷ .7 =

```
      8.57
.7)60.00
   - 56
     4 0
    - 3 5
       50
      - 49
        1
```
8.57 rounds to 8.6

2.
10 ÷ 1.3 =

3.
12 ÷ 4.1 =

4.
4 ÷ 2.2 =

Divide. Round to the nearest hundredth.

5.
50 ÷ .75 =

6.
100 ÷ 6.49 =

7.
29 ÷ 10.8 =

8.
76 ÷ 4.3 =

Dividing Decimals by Decimals

To divide a decimal by another decimal, you need to move the decimal points in both numbers the same number of places to the right. You may need to add zeros to the number you are dividing into.

Use These Steps

Divide 5.25 ÷ .75

1. Set up the problem.

$$.75 \overline{)5.25}$$

2. Move both decimal points two places to the right. Put a decimal point in the answer.

$$.75 \overline{)5.25} \\ \, \curvearrowright \quad \curvearrowright$$

3. Divide.

$$\begin{array}{r} 7. \\ 75 \overline{)525} \\ -525 \\ \hline 0 \end{array}$$

Divide.

1.

.91 ÷ .7 =

$$\begin{array}{r} 1.3 \\ .7 \overline{).91} \\ \curvearrowright \, \curvearrowright \\ -7 \\ \hline 21 \\ -21 \\ \hline 0 \end{array}$$

2.

5.4 ÷ .3 =

3.

8.2 ÷ 4.1 =

4.

26.4 ÷ .24 =

5.

.36 ÷ .6 =

6.

9.7 ÷ .5 =

7.

29.43 ÷ 2.7 =

8.

.76 ÷ 1.9 =

9.

$$.22 \overline{).352}$$

10.

$$3.4 \overline{)21.42}$$

11.

$$.15 \overline{)4.83}$$

12.

$$.72 \overline{)1.512}$$

Dividing Decimals by Decimals

Remember to move both decimal points the same number of places before dividing.

Use These Steps

Divide 2.3 ÷ .6 Round to the nearest hundredth.

1. Set up the problem.

2. Move both decimal points one place to the right. Put a decimal point in the answer.

3. Divide. Add zeros. Round to the nearest hundredth.

$.6\overline{)2.3}$

$.6\overline{)2.3}$

```
     3.833
  6)23.000
   −18
     5 0
   − 4 8
       20
     − 18
        20
      − 18
         2
```

3.833 rounds to 3.83

Divide. Round to the nearest tenth.

1.

.75 ÷ 1.3 =

```
      .57
1.3).750
   − 65
    100
   −  91
      9
```

.57 rounds to .6

2.

.348 ÷ .9 =

3.

18.5 ÷ .239 =

4.

2.61 ÷ .4 =

Divide. Round to the nearest hundredth.

5.

67.6 ÷ 3.22 =

6.

.881 ÷ .25 =

7.

7.47 ÷ 2.4 =

8.

3.143 ÷ .5 =

Problem Solving: Using Estimating

Often you do not need to find the exact answer to a problem. Estimating will give you an answer that is close to the exact answer. You are estimating when you round a decimal to the nearest whole number.

Example Mrs. Blake delivers mail 6 days a week for the Oakmont Post Office. One week, she drove 23.62 miles delivering mail. About how many miles did she average each day?

▶ **Step 1.** Estimate by rounding 23.62 to the nearest whole number.

23.62 rounds to 24.

▶ **Step 2.** Divide 24 by 6.

$$\begin{array}{r} 4 \\ 6\overline{)24} \\ -24 \\ \hline 0 \end{array}$$

Mrs. Blake averaged about 4 miles each day.

Round each amount to the nearest whole number if necessary. Then solve.

1. The Oakmont Post Office has 14 mail carriers. Each day they drive 69.7 miles delivering mail. On the average, how many miles does each mail carrier drive a day?

   Answer_____

2. One day only 10 mail carriers were available to cover the 69.7 miles. If the mail carriers divided the 69.7 miles equally, about how many miles did each carrier drive?

   Answer_____

3. Mr. Johnson carries mail part time for the Oakmont Post Office. If he walks 4.2 miles in 2.15 hours, about how fast is he walking?

   Answer_____

4. Part of Mr. Johnson's job is to sort mail. If he sorted 1,034 pieces of mail among 200 households, on the average, how many pieces of mail did each household receive?
   (Hint: Round the answer to the nearest whole number.)

   Answer_____

5. Ms. Smith waits on customers at the post office. If a customer paid $7.10 for 22 stamps for postcards and letters, what was the average cost per stamp, rounded to the nearest cent?

Answer_____

6. Mr. Pena mailed 5 identical packages last week. If the total cost of mailing the packages was $19.92, about how much did he pay for postage per package?

Answer_____

7. Mrs. White worked 31.5 hours last week at the post office. If she worked 4 days, about how many hours did she work each day?

Answer_____

8. Mrs. White's paycheck at the end of one week was $210.25. About how much did she make per hour if she worked 29.5 hours that week?

Answer_____

9. Mr. Jones drives 21.9 miles round trip each day to go to his job at the post office and to go back home again. About how far does he live from the post office?

Answer_____

10. Mr. Jones carried about 140 pounds of mail in his mail truck one day during the holidays. If he delivered mail to 100 customers, what was the average weight of each customer's mail?

Answer_____

Unit 3 *Review*

Multiply.

1. $\$.67 \times 4 =$

2. $\$.99 \times 6 =$

3. $\$7.49 \times 5 =$

4. $\$1.35 \times 8 =$

5. $\$11.87 \times 12 =$

6. $\$69.98 \times 24 =$

7. $\$.50 \times 100 =$

8. $\$2.95 \times 1,000 =$

9. $.8 \times 6 =$

10. $3.2 \times 7 =$

11. $.06 \times 9 =$

12. $15.29 \times 5 =$

13. $1.201 \times 25 =$

14. $.851 \times 14 =$

15. $21.03 \times 10 =$

16. $.34 \times 1,000 =$

17. $3.2 \times 1.4 =$

18. $10.05 \times .33 =$

19. $.7 \times .9 =$

20. $12.3 \times 4.27 =$

21. $.2 \times .1 =$

22. $.05 \times .3 =$

23. $.3 \times .9 =$

24. $2.3 \times .08 =$

Divide.

25. $\$9.20 \div 4 =$

26. $\$14.00 \div 8 =$

27. $\$.95 \div 5 =$

28. $\$46.92 \div 17 =$

Divide. Round each answer to the nearest hundredth.

29.
$200.00 ÷ 10 =

30.
$ .98 ÷ 10 =

31.
$3.47 ÷ 100 =

32.
$92.06 ÷ 1,000 =

33.
.40 ÷ 8 =

34.
2.42 ÷ 11 =

35.
.379 ÷ 42 =

36.
31.84 ÷ 6 =

37.
2.1 ÷ 10 =

38.
17.37 ÷ 100 =

39.
416.9 ÷ 100 =

40.
.2 ÷ 1,000 =

41.
124 ÷ .4 =

42.
28 ÷ .36 =

43.
2.9 ÷ 1.4 =

44.
8.906 ÷ .15 =

Below is a list of the problems in this review and the pages on which the skills are taught. If you missed any problems, turn to the pages listed and practice the skills. Then correct the problems you missed in the Unit Review.

Problems	Pages	Problems	Pages
1-8	49-51	33-36	62-63
9-16	52-54	37-40	64
17-24	55-56	41-42	65-66
25-32	59-61	43-44	67-68

You must understand the meaning of ratios, proportions, and percents before you can work with percent problems. Percents, like fractions and decimals, are used to show part of a whole. For example, if you have $20 and you spend $10, you have spent $\frac{10}{20}$ or 50% of your money.

In this unit, you will learn how to write ratios, proportions, and percents. You will learn how to change from fractions to decimals and to percents and how to change from percents to decimals and to fractions.

Getting Ready

You should be familiar with the skills on this page and the next before you begin this unit.

 You will need to use place value when working with percents.

Write the place value of the underlined digit in each number.

1. 13.2 _____two tenths_____

2. 1.32<u>4</u>5 _____

3. .0<u>7</u> _____

4. 29.03<u>6</u> _____

5. 9.0<u>0</u>8 _____

6. 6.<u>9</u>8 _____

For review, see Unit 1, page 19.

To change a fraction to a decimal, divide the numerator by the denominator. Divide until there is no remainder.

Change each fraction to a decimal.

7.
$$\frac{1}{2} = .5$$

$$\begin{array}{r} .5 \\ 2\overline{)1.0} \\ -1\,0 \\ \hline 0 \end{array}$$

8.
$$\frac{3}{4} =$$

9.
$$\frac{2}{5} =$$

10.
$$\frac{3}{10} =$$

11.
$$\frac{1}{20} =$$

12.
$$\frac{3}{5} =$$

13.
$$\frac{9}{20} =$$

14.
$$\frac{4}{25} =$$

For review, see Unit 1, page 21.

 When changing some fractions to decimals, your answer may have a remainder.

Change each fraction to a decimal with two digits to the right of the decimal point. Write the remainder as a fraction.

15.
$$\frac{1}{3} = .33\frac{1}{3}$$

$$\begin{array}{r} .33\frac{1}{3} \\ 3\overline{)1.00} \\ -9 \\ \hline 10 \\ -9 \\ \hline 1 \end{array}$$

16.
$$\frac{5}{6} =$$

17.
$$\frac{4}{9} =$$

18.
$$\frac{2}{3} =$$

19.
$$\frac{7}{15} =$$

20.
$$\frac{5}{18} =$$

21.
$$\frac{2}{11} =$$

22.
$$\frac{3}{7} =$$

For review, see Unit 1, page 22.

Ratios

A ratio is a fraction that shows a relationship between two numbers. For example, if there are 4 cashiers and 27 customers, then the ratio of cashiers to customers can be shown as the fraction $\frac{4}{27}$.

Always write the first number in the relationship as the numerator and the second number as the denominator.

Look at the examples below. Notice that the denominators may be smaller than the numerators.

5 hits out of 9 times at bat = $\frac{5}{9}$ 70 pitches in 6 innings = $\frac{70}{6}$ 1 win and 1 loss = $\frac{1}{1}$

A ratio may be reduced without changing the relationship. It can have a denominator of 1, but it cannot be changed to a mixed number or a whole number.

Use These Steps

Write a ratio to show a car traveling 48 miles on 3 gallons of gas.

1. Write the first number in the relationship as the numerator of the fraction.

   $\frac{48}{}$

2. Write the second number as the denominator.

   $\frac{48}{3}$

3. Reduce.

   $\frac{48 \div 3}{3 \div 3} = \frac{16}{1}$

Write a ratio for each problem. Reduce if possible.

1. 7 out of 10 houses

   $\frac{7}{10}$

2. 6 sodas for 9 people

3. 99 out of 100 doctors

4. 50 yards in 10 seconds

   $\frac{50}{10} = \frac{50 \div 10}{10 \div 10} = \frac{5}{1}$

5. 2 pain relievers in 1 pill

6. 5 fingers on 1 hand

7. 6 muffins for 6 people

8. 4 wins and 4 losses

9. 2 out of 3 dentists

10. Richard worked 8 hours on Saturday and 5 hours on Sunday. What is the ratio of the number of hours he worked on Saturday to the hours he worked on Sunday?

11. Mrs. Salk prepared 200 dinners for a graduation banquet. Only 194 guests went to the banquet. Write the ratio of dinners she prepared to the number of guests at the banquet.

Answer _____

Answer _____

Equal Ratios

You can change ratios to higher terms by multiplying both the numerator and the denominator by the same number. For example, if you can buy 3 oranges for \$1, $\frac{3}{1}$, you can buy 6 oranges for \$2, $\frac{6}{2}$, because $\frac{3}{1} = \frac{6}{2}$.

You can use cross-multiplication to determine if two ratios are equal. To cross-multiply, multiply the numbers in the opposite corners. If the ratios are equal, the answers to the cross-multiplication will be equal.

Use These Steps

Change $\frac{7}{2}$ to an equal ratio with 6 as the denominator.

1. Raise $\frac{7}{2}$ to higher terms with a denominator of 6.

$$\frac{7}{2} = \frac{7 \times 3}{2 \times 3} = \frac{21}{6}$$

2. Check by cross-multiplication.

$$\frac{7}{2} \bowtie \frac{21}{6}$$
$$7 \times 6 = 2 \times 21$$
$$42 = 42$$

Change to higher terms. Check by cross-multiplication.

1.
$$\frac{3}{8} = \frac{\boxed{6}}{16}$$
$$\frac{3}{8} = \frac{3 \times 2}{8 \times 2} = \frac{6}{16}$$
Check:
$$\frac{3}{8} \bowtie \frac{6}{16}$$
$$3 \times 16 = 8 \times 6$$
$$48 = 48$$

2.
$$\frac{4}{9} = \frac{\boxed{}}{27}$$

3.
$$\frac{7}{10} = \frac{\boxed{}}{20}$$

4.
$$\frac{5}{6} = \frac{\boxed{}}{36}$$

5.
$$\frac{1}{2} = \frac{2}{\boxed{}}$$

6.
$$\frac{2}{3} = \frac{6}{\boxed{}}$$

7.
$$\frac{4}{7} = \frac{8}{\boxed{}}$$

8.
$$\frac{3}{5} = \frac{9}{\boxed{}}$$

9. Mrs. Hartman can correct 2 tests in 5 minutes. How much time does she need to correct 16 tests?

10. If the computer prints 2 tests in 3 minutes, how many tests can it print in 15 minutes?

Answer _____

Answer _____

Equal Ratios

Equal ratios are equal fractions. If the numerator or the denominator is missing from one fraction, you can find it by multiplying (changing to higher terms) or dividing (reducing to lower terms). Write *n* to show a missing number.

$$\frac{n}{2} = \frac{1}{2}$$

Use These Steps

Find n. $\frac{n}{12} = \frac{2}{3}$

1. To find the missing number, n, change $\frac{2}{3}$ to an equal ratio with a denominator of 12.

$$\frac{n}{12} = \frac{2}{3}$$

$$\frac{2}{3} = \frac{2 \times 4}{3 \times 4} = \frac{8}{12}$$

$$n = 8$$

2. Check by cross-multiplication.

$$\frac{8}{12} \bowtie \frac{2}{3}$$

$$8 \times 3 = 12 \times 2$$
$$24 = 24$$

Find n. Check by cross-multiplication.

1.

$$\frac{2}{6} = \frac{n}{3}$$

$$\frac{2}{6} = \frac{2 \div 2}{6 \div 2} = \frac{1}{3}$$

$$n = 1$$

Check:

$$\frac{2}{6} \bowtie \frac{1}{3}$$

$$2 \times 3 = 6 \times 1$$
$$6 = 6$$

2.

$$\frac{n}{20} = \frac{4}{5}$$

3.

$$\frac{9}{21} = \frac{3}{n}$$

4.

$$\frac{n}{8} = \frac{3}{4}$$

5.

$$\frac{n}{4} = \frac{3}{12}$$

6.

$$\frac{5}{n} = \frac{10}{12}$$

7.

$$\frac{4}{14} = \frac{n}{7}$$

8.

$$\frac{4}{n} = \frac{20}{25}$$

9. Darryl's Electronics rents 3 DVDs for $6. How many DVDs do they rent for $2?

Answer_____

10. Darryl's rents a DVD player for 2 days for $5. How much does it cost to rent a DVD player for 4 days?

Answer_____

Proportions

Equal ratios are called proportions. Proportions are used to solve problems when the relationship between two things does not change. For example, if you know that your car uses 1 gallon of gas to go 24 miles, you can find out how many gallons of gas you need to go 240 miles by writing a proportion and cross multiplying to find the missing number.

$$\frac{1 \text{ gallon}}{24 \text{ miles}} = \frac{n \text{ gallons}}{240 \text{ miles}}$$

When you cross-multiply, first multiply n by the number in the opposite corner. Then write the answer on the left side of the equal sign.

$$24 \times n = 1 \times 240$$

Use These Steps

Find n. $\frac{1}{2} = \frac{n}{24}$

1. Cross-multiply. 2n means 2 times n.

$$\frac{1}{2} \bowtie \frac{n}{24}$$

$$2 \times n = 1 \times 24$$
$$2n = 24$$

2. Divide the number on the right of the equal sign by the number next to n, 2.

$$n = 24 \div 2 = 12$$

3. Check by substituting the answer, 12, for n. Cross-multiply.

$$\frac{1}{2} \bowtie \frac{12}{24}$$

$$2 \times 12 = 1 \times 24$$
$$24 = 24$$

Find n. Check by substituting the answer and cross-multiplying.

1.
$$\frac{n}{5} \bowtie \frac{6}{15}$$
$$n \times 15 = 5 \times 6$$
$$15n = 30$$
$$n = 30 \div 15 = 2$$
Check:
$$\frac{2}{5} \bowtie \frac{6}{15}$$
$$2 \times 15 = 5 \times 6$$
$$30 = 30$$

2. $\frac{3}{4} = \frac{12}{n}$

3. $\frac{n}{9} = \frac{1}{3}$

4. $\frac{3}{n} = \frac{15}{25}$

5. $\frac{3}{24} = \frac{n}{8}$

6. $\frac{n}{32} = \frac{15}{16}$

7. $\frac{7}{10} = \frac{21}{n}$

8. $\frac{n}{4} = \frac{25}{100}$

Application

Proportions are especially useful for solving problems that you cannot do easily in your head.

Example If 2 grapefruit cost $ .75, how much do 3 grapefruit cost?

$$\frac{2 \text{ grapefruit}}{\$ .75} = \frac{3 \text{ grapefruit}}{n}$$

$$2 \times n = \$.75 \times 3$$
$$2n = \$2.25$$
$$n = \$2.25 \div 2 = \$1.125$$

Round the answer to the nearest hundredth, or cent.

$1.125 rounds to $1.13, so 3 grapefruit cost $1.13.

Write a proportion. Solve. Round the answers to the nearest hundredth, or cent.

1. If cucumbers are 2 for $ .75, how much do 9 cucumbers cost?

2. If bananas are 3 pounds for $1.25, how much do 4 pounds cost?

Answer_____

Answer_____

3. If tomatoes are 5 pounds for $3.00, how much do 2 pounds cost?

4. If lemons are 3 for $1.00, how much do 10 lemons cost?

Answer_____

Answer_____

Mixed Review

Write a ratio for each problem. Reduce if possible.

1. 2 coupons to a customer
2. 18 socks to 24 shoes
3. 4 chances out of 100
4. 3 pounds for $1
5. 85 miles in 2 hours
6. 10 trucks to 10 drivers

Find n by reducing or changing to higher terms. Check by cross-multiplying.

7. $\frac{1}{3} = \frac{n}{6}$

8. $\frac{3}{27} = \frac{n}{9}$

9. $\frac{8}{10} = \frac{4}{n}$

10. $\frac{5}{6} = \frac{30}{n}$

11. $\frac{n}{40} = \frac{3}{8}$

12. $\frac{n}{7} = \frac{21}{49}$

13. $\frac{16}{n} = \frac{4}{5}$

14. $\frac{3}{n} = \frac{12}{100}$

Find n by cross-multiplying. Check by substituting the answer and cross-multiplying.

15. $\frac{1}{4} = \frac{n}{24}$

16. $\frac{9}{n} = \frac{3}{20}$

17. $\frac{n}{10} = \frac{2}{5}$

18. $\frac{4}{n} = \frac{2}{7}$

19. $\frac{n}{10} = \frac{1}{2}$

20. $\frac{5}{10} = \frac{n}{100}$

21. $\frac{15}{n} = \frac{3}{24}$

22. $\frac{4}{8} = \frac{1}{n}$

23. Capital Cars rents a compact car for 3 days for $132. How much does it cost to rent the car for 1 day?

24. A mid-size car rents for 5 days for $300. How much does it cost to rent the car for 2 days?

Answer_____

Answer_____

Writing Percents

Percent means hundredths. When using percents, the whole is divided into 100 equal parts. Twenty-five percent (25%) means 25 hundredths or 25 out of 100 parts. The sign % is read *percent*.

25%
twenty-five percent

100%
one hundred percent

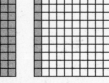

110%
one hundred ten percent

Use These Steps

Write ten percent using the percent sign.

1. Write ten.

10

2. Write the percent sign after the 10.

10%

Write each percent using the percent sign.

1. five percent = 5%

2. eight percent =

3. two percent =

4. seven percent =

5. sixteen percent =

6. twenty-four percent =

7. thirty-nine percent =

8. forty-one percent =

9. sixty percent =

10. fifty percent =

11. eighty percent =

12. one hundred percent =

13. four and one half percent = $4\frac{1}{2}\%$

14. thirty-three and one third percent =

15. two hundred forty-five percent =

16. thirteen percent =

17. two and three tenths percent =

18. twenty and one half percent =

Write a percent for each figure.

19.

2%

20.

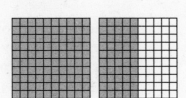

21.

22.

Changing Percents to Decimals

You can write any percent as a decimal by writing the number without the percent sign and moving the decimal point two places to the left. Remember that you can drop a zero at the end of a decimal without changing its value.

$$50\% = 50 = .5 \qquad 36\% = 36 = .36 \qquad 12\% = 12 = .12$$

For percents less than 10%, put a zero in front of the number so that you can move the decimal point two places to the left.

$$1\% = 01 = .01 \qquad 5\% = 05 = .05 \qquad 9\% = 09 = .09$$

Use These Steps

Change 75% to a decimal.

1. Write the number without the percent sign.

   75

2. Move the decimal point two places to the left.

   75 = .75

Change each percent to a decimal.

1. $35\% = 35 = .35$

2. $19\% =$

3. $27\% =$

4. $42\% =$

5. $10\% = 10 = .10 = .1$

6. $30\% =$

7. $70\% =$

8. $90\% =$

9. $6\% = 06 = .06$

10. $1\% =$

11. $3\% =$

12. $9\% =$

13. $29\% =$

14. $4\% =$

15. $40\% =$

16. $72\% =$

17. $54\% =$

18. $2\% =$

19. $41\% =$

20. $66\% =$

21. Mr. Marcos spends 25% of his work day working for a messenger service. Write as a decimal the part of each work day he spends working for the messenger service.

22. The other 75% of his work day, Mr. Marcos plays drums for a band. Write as a decimal the part of the work day he plays in the band.

Answer_____

Answer_____

Changing Percents Greater Than 100% to Decimals

If you have 100% of something, you have the whole thing. Sometimes, however, you will have percents greater than 100%. To change percents greater than 100% to a decimal, write the number without the percent sign and move the decimal two places to the left.

$200\% = 200 = 2.00 = 2$ $250\% = 250 = 2.50 = 2.5$ $309\% = 309 = 3.09$

Use These Steps

Change 120% to a decimal.

1. Write the number without the percent sign.

2. Move the decimal point two places to the left. Drop the zero at the end.

120

$1\,20 = 1.20 = 1.2$

Change each percent to a decimal.

1.
$300\% = 300 = 3.00 = 3$

2.
$500\% =$

3.
$700\% =$

4.
$270\% = 270 = 2.70 = 2.7$

5.
$110\% =$

6.
$450\% =$

7.
$107\% = 107 = 1.07$

8.
$308\% =$

9.
$701\% =$

10.
$925\% =$

11.
$714\% =$

12.
$283\% =$

13.
$520\% =$

14.
$624\% =$

15.
$800\% =$

16.
$135\% =$

17.
$470\% =$

18.
$209\% =$

19. There was a 212% increase in the number of houses sold last year. Write 212% as a decimal.

20. A construction company built 145% more new houses this year than last year. Write 145% as a decimal.

Answer _____

Answer _____

Changing Complex Percents to Decimals

A complex percent has a whole number and a fraction. To change a complex percent to a decimal, change the fraction to a decimal. Then move the decimal point two places to the left. Add a zero if necessary.

$$6\frac{1}{2}\% = 6.5\% = 06.5 = .065$$

Some complex percents do not have exact decimal equivalents. When you divide to change the percent to a decimal, you will always have a remainder. Write the remainder as a fraction.

$$33\frac{1}{3}\% = 33\frac{1}{3} = .33\frac{1}{3}$$

Use These Steps

Change $10\frac{1}{2}\%$ to a decimal.

1. Change the fraction to a decimal.	2. Write the number without the percent sign.	3. Move the decimal point two places to the left.
$10\frac{1}{2}\% = 10.5\%$	10.5	$10.5 = .105$

Change each percent to a decimal.

1.
$$2\frac{1}{4}\% = 2.25\% = 02.25 = .0225$$

2.
$$3\frac{1}{10}\% =$$

3.
$$6\frac{1}{2}\% =$$

4.
$$7\frac{1}{3}\% = 07\frac{1}{3} = .07\frac{1}{3}$$

5.
$$10\frac{2}{3}\% =$$

6.
$$2\frac{1}{5}\% =$$

7.
$$30\frac{1}{2}\% =$$

8.
$$16\frac{3}{10}\% =$$

9.
$$50\frac{1}{5}\% =$$

10.
$$8\frac{1}{2}\% =$$

11.
$$22\frac{1}{10}\% =$$

12.
$$1\frac{21}{25}\% =$$

13.
$$9\frac{9}{10}\% =$$

14.
$$2\frac{4}{5}\% =$$

15.
$$25\frac{4}{25}\% =$$

Application

When people borrow money from a bank or credit union, they must pay interest on the money they borrow. When they save money, the bank or credit union pays them interest on the money they save. Sometimes the bank or credit union pays them interest on the money in their checking account. Interest is figured using a rate or percent.

Example The interest rate for a four-year new car loan is $9\frac{1}{4}\%$ at National Bank. The interest rate at Western Bank is 9.5%. Which bank has the lower interest rate?

$9\frac{1}{4}\% = 09.25 = .0925$

$9.5\% = 09.5 = .095$

$.0925 < .095$, so $9\frac{1}{4}\% < 9.5\%$.

The interest rate at National Bank is lower.

Solve.

1. The interest rate for a used-car loan for four years at National Bank is $10\frac{1}{2}\%$. The interest rate at Western Bank is 10.25%. Which bank has the lower interest rate?

    Answer_____

2. The interest rate for a used-car loan for three years at National Bank is $10\frac{3}{4}\%$. The interest rate at Western Bank is 10.5%. Which bank has the lower interest rate?

    Answer_____

3. The interest rate for a thirty-year conventional home loan at National Bank is $8\frac{1}{4}\%$. The interest rate at Western Bank is 8.75%. Which bank has the lower interest rate?

    Answer_____

4. The interest rate for a thirty-year home loan at National Bank is $8\frac{1}{4}\%$. The interest rate at Western Bank is 8.125%. Which bank has the lower interest rate?

    Answer_____

Changing Decimals to Percents

To change a decimal to a percent, move the decimal point two places to the right. This is the same as multiplying by 100. You may need to add a zero to the end of the number. Add a percent sign.

$$.06 = .06 = 6\% \qquad .5 = .50 = 50\% \qquad .66\tfrac{2}{3} = .66\tfrac{2}{3} = 66\tfrac{2}{3}\%$$

Use These Steps

Change .2 to a percent.

1. Add a zero.

    .2 = .20

2. Move the decimal point two places to the right.

    .20 = .20 = 20

3. Add a percent sign.

    20%

Change each decimal to a percent.

1. $.01 = .01 = 1\%$

2. $.07 =$

3. $.09 =$

4. $.05 =$

5. $.1 = .10 = 10\%$

6. $.3 =$

7. $.6 =$

8. $.9 =$

9. $.25 =$

10. $.75 =$

11. $.47 =$

12. $.65 =$

13. $.865 =$

14. $.031 =$

15. $.799 =$

16. $.209 =$

17. $.33\tfrac{1}{3} = .33\tfrac{1}{3} = 33\tfrac{1}{3}\%$

18. $.16\tfrac{2}{3} =$

19. $.83\tfrac{1}{3} =$

20. $.16\tfrac{2}{3} =$

21. $.99 =$

22. $.08 =$

23. $.074 =$

24. $.5 =$

25. $.033 =$

26. $.7 =$

27. $.06 =$

28. $.225 =$

Application

Many real-life situations use percents. Taxes are figured using percents. Some sale prices are shown as a "percent off." Interest on loans and savings accounts is a percent of the amount borrowed or saved.

Example   An employee and his employer contribute a total of 15% of his wages for social security. Write this amount as a decimal.

$$15\% = 15 = .15$$

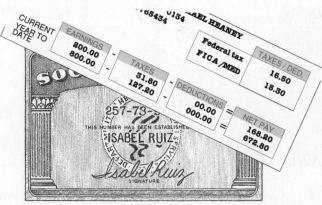

Write each percent as a decimal.

1. Some people pay 28% of their taxable income for income taxes.

   Answer_____

2. Sales tax in one large city is 8%.

   Answer_____

3. Gasoline tax in one state is 22%.

   Answer_____

4. At last week's sale, Janie saved 25%.

   Answer_____

5. Barbara earns 5% interest on her savings account.

   Answer_____

6. Mr. Sayres pays 16% interest on his credit card.

   Answer_____

7. Oscar's brother pays 9% interest on his student loan.

   Answer_____

8. Ms. Julian makes 3% commission on each car she sells.

   Answer_____

9. Jan saves 10% of the money she earns.

   Answer_____

10. Lyla got a 4% raise this year.

    Answer_____

Mixed Review

Write a ratio for each problem. Reduce if possible.

1.
   3 tables to 12 chairs

2.
   9 buses for 180 children

3.
   5 pounds for \$3

4.
   4 tires for 1 car

Solve each proportion for n.

5. $\frac{3}{7} = \frac{n}{14}$

6. $\frac{2}{n} = \frac{1}{9}$

7. $\frac{4}{5} = \frac{12}{n}$

8. $\frac{n}{25} = \frac{12}{5}$

Write each percent with the percent sign.

9. twenty-five percent =

10. one hundred percent =

11. two and one half percent =

12. thirty percent =

Change each percent to a decimal.

13. $29\% =$

14. $8\% =$

15. $2\frac{1}{2}\% =$

16. $1\frac{9}{10}\% =$

17. $7.2\% =$

18. $75\% =$

19. $120\% =$

20. $406\% =$

21. $5\frac{1}{2}\% =$

22. $8\frac{1}{3}\% =$

23. $10\frac{2}{3}\% =$

24. $19.5\% =$

Change each decimal to a percent.

25. $.8 =$

26. $.05 =$

27. $.16 =$

28. $.425 =$

29. $.1 =$

30. $.75 =$

31. $.081 =$

32. $.01 =$

33. $.506 =$

34. $.22 =$

35. $.6 =$

36. $.947 =$

Application

Many statistics in sports are given in percents. The batting averages in baseball are really percents. The chart to the right shows the batting averages of several baseball players. Batting averages are written with three decimal places.

Batting Averages	Player	Hits	Times at Bat	Average	Percent
	Ruiz, J	35	125	.280	28%
	Lee, A.	4	20		
	Delsanto, S.	18	75		
	Montoya, B.	3	12		
	Shaffer, T.	7	25		

Example Ruiz has a ratio of 35 hits out of 125 times at bat. What is Ruiz's batting average? What is the percent?

$$\frac{\text{hits}}{\text{times at bat}} = \frac{35}{125}$$

$$\frac{35}{125} = 35 \div 125$$

$$35 \div 125 = .28$$

$$.28 = .28 = 28\%$$

Ruiz has a batting average of .280 and a percent of 28%.

Solve. Fill in the chart.

1. What is Lee's batting average? What is the percent?

   Answer_____

2. What is Delsanto's batting average? What is the percent?

   Answer_____

3. What is Montoya's batting average? What is the percent?

   Answer_____

4. What is Shaffer's batting average? What is the percent?

   Answer_____

Changing Percents to Fractions

For some percent problems, it may be easier to change the percent to a fraction instead of to a decimal.

Since percent means hundredths, to change a percent to a fraction, write the number over 100 without the percent sign. When you have a percent greater than 100%, you will get an improper fraction.

$$25\% = \frac{25}{100} = \frac{1}{4} \qquad 37\% = \frac{37}{100} \qquad 250\% = \frac{250}{100} = \frac{5}{2}$$

Change 50% to a fraction.

1. Write the number over 100 without the percent sign.

$$50\% = \frac{50}{100}$$

2. Reduce.

$$\frac{5\!\!\!/0}{10\!\!\!/0} = \frac{5}{10} = \frac{1}{2}$$

Change each percent to a fraction. Reduce if possible.

1. $75\% = \frac{75}{100} = \frac{3}{4}$

2. $16\% =$

3. $45\% =$

4. $99\% =$

5. $30\% =$

6. $50\% =$

7. $6\% =$

8. $2\% =$

9. $5\% =$

10. $25\% =$

11. $40\% =$

12. $83\% =$

Change each percent to an improper fraction. Reduce if possible.

13. $300\% = \frac{300}{100} = \frac{3}{1}$

14. $500\% =$

15. $870\% =$

16. $225\% =$

17. $460\% =$

18. $986\% =$

19. $200\% =$

20. $670\% =$

21. Last year Koji sold magazine subscriptions to 60% of the people he contacted. Express as a fraction the percent of subscriptions sold to people contacted.

22. This year, Koji increased his sales by 120%. Express as a fraction the percent of increased sales.

Answer_____

Answer_____

Changing Complex Percents to Fractions

When you change a complex percent to a fraction, write the mixed number over 100 without the percent sign. Divide the numerator by the denominator.

Use These Steps

Change $3\frac{1}{3}\%$ to a fraction.

1. Write the mixed number over 100 without the percent sign. Set up a division problem.

$$3\frac{1}{3}\% = \frac{3\frac{1}{3}}{100} = 3\frac{1}{3} \div 100$$

2. Change both numbers to improper fractions. Invert and multiply. Reduce.

$$3\frac{1}{3} \div 100 = \frac{10}{3} \div \frac{100}{1} = \frac{\overset{1}{\cancel{10}}}{3} \times \frac{1}{\underset{10}{\cancel{100}}} = \frac{1}{30}$$

Change each percent to a fraction.

1.

$$7\frac{1}{2}\% =$$

$$\frac{7\frac{1}{2}}{100} = 7\frac{1}{2} \div 100 = \frac{15}{2} \div \frac{100}{1} = \frac{\overset{3}{\cancel{15}}}{2} \times \frac{1}{\underset{20}{\cancel{100}}} = \frac{3}{40}$$

2.

$$12\frac{1}{2}\% =$$

3.

$$8\frac{1}{3}\% =$$

4.

$$66\frac{2}{3}\% =$$

5.

$$16\frac{2}{3}\% =$$

6.

$$33\frac{1}{3}\% =$$

7.

$$1\frac{1}{4}\% =$$

8.

$$3\frac{3}{4}\% =$$

9.

$$3\frac{1}{8}\% =$$

10.

$$9\frac{3}{8}\% =$$

Changing Fractions to Percents

To change a fraction to a percent, first change the fraction to a decimal by dividing the numerator by the denominator. Move the decimal point two places to the right and add a percent sign.

Use These Steps

Change $\frac{3}{4}$ to a percent.

1. Change the fraction to a decimal by dividing the numerator by the denominator. Divide until there is no remainder.

$$
\begin{array}{r}
.75 \\
4\overline{)3.00} \\
-28 \\
\hline
20 \\
-20 \\
\hline
0
\end{array}
$$

2. Move the decimal point two places to the right. Add a percent sign.

$$.75 = .75 = 75\%$$

Change each fraction to a percent.

1. $\frac{1}{2} =$

$$
\begin{array}{r}
.5 \\
2\overline{)1.0} \\
-10 \\
\hline
0
\end{array}
$$

$.5 = .50 = 50\%$

2. $\frac{3}{15} =$

3. $\frac{2}{5} =$

4. $\frac{7}{10} =$

5. $\frac{9}{25} =$

6. $\frac{7}{20} =$

7. $\frac{3}{20} =$

8. $\frac{7}{25} =$

9. $\frac{1}{5} =$

10. $\frac{16}{25} =$

11. $\frac{1}{4} =$

12. $\frac{3}{10} =$

13. $\frac{9}{10} =$

14. $\frac{3}{5} =$

15. $\frac{9}{150} =$

16. $\frac{3}{100} =$

Changing Fractions to Percents

When changed to decimals, some fractions will always have a remainder. When this happens, keep only two places in the answer and write the remainder as a fraction. Then move the decimal point two places to the right and add a percent sign.

Use These Steps

Change $\frac{1}{3}$ to a percent.

1. Change the fraction to a decimal with two places by dividing the numerator by the denominator. Write the remainder as a fraction.

$$
\begin{array}{r}
.33\frac{1}{3} \\
3\overline{)1.00} \\
-\ 9 \\
\hline
10 \\
-\ 9 \\
\hline
1
\end{array}
$$

2. Move the decimal point two places to the right. Add a percent sign.

$$.33\frac{1}{3} = .33\frac{1}{3} = 33\frac{1}{3}\%$$

Change each fraction to a percent. Reduce if possible.

1. $\frac{2}{3} =$

$$
\begin{array}{r}
.66\frac{2}{3} \\
3\overline{)2.00} \\
-\ 1\ 8 \\
\hline
20 \\
-\ 18 \\
\hline
2
\end{array}
$$

$$.66\frac{2}{3} = .66\frac{2}{3} = 66\frac{2}{3}\%$$

2. $\frac{7}{12} =$

3. $\frac{4}{9} =$

4. $\frac{5}{12} =$

5. $\frac{5}{6} =$

6. $\frac{8}{9} =$

7. $\frac{1}{15} =$

8. $\frac{11}{12} =$

Fractions, Decimals, and Percents

You will find it helpful to memorize these commonly used equivalent fractions, decimals, and percents. This will save you some work when doing problems with percents.

Fill in the chart below.

Fraction	Decimal	Percent
$\frac{1}{100}$	.01	1%
$\frac{1}{10}$		
$\frac{1}{8}$	.125	$12\frac{1}{2}\%$
$\frac{1}{6}$	$.16\frac{2}{3}$	$16\frac{2}{3}\%$
$\frac{1}{5}$		
$\frac{1}{4}$		
$\frac{3}{10}$		
$\frac{1}{3}$		
$\frac{3}{8}$		
$\frac{2}{5}$		
$\frac{1}{2}$		
$\frac{3}{5}$		
$\frac{5}{8}$		
$\frac{2}{3}$		
$\frac{7}{10}$		
$\frac{3}{4}$		
$\frac{5}{6}$		
$\frac{7}{8}$		
$\frac{9}{10}$		
1	1.0	100%

Comparing Decimals and Percents

If you want to compare a decimal and a percent, they must be in the same form.

Remember the symbol < means *less than*.
> means *greater than*.

Use These Steps

Compare .2 ☐ 25%

1. You can change .2 to a percent or you can change 25% to a decimal.

   .2 = .20 = 20%
   ⌣
   or
   25% = 25 = .25
   ⌣

2. Compare the new forms.

   20% < 25%, so .2 < 25%

   or
   .2 < .25, so .2 < 25%

Change each pair of numbers to the same form. Then compare. Use <, >, or =.

1.
14% $\boxed{<}$ 2.1
14% = 14 = .14
⌣
.14 < 2.1, so 14% < 2.1

2.
104% $\boxed{<}$ 1.4
1.4 = 1.40 = 140%
⌣
104% < 140%, so 104% < 1.4

3.
8% ☐ .026

4.
205% ☐ .25

5.
36% ☐ .36

6.
70% ☐ .9

7.
.06 ☐ 2.6%

8.
1.37 ☐ 14.2%

9.
.875 ☐ 75%

10.
1.3 ☐ 158%

11.
6.2 ☐ $62\frac{1}{2}$%

12.
.013 ☐ 13%

13.
.125 ☐ $12\frac{1}{2}$%

14.
.31 ☐ 31%

15.
12.3 ☐ 1.5%

16.
.6 ☐ 60%

Comparing Fractions and Percents

Fractions and percents must be in the same form if you want to compare them. The easiest way to compare fractions and percents is to change each number to a decimal.

Compare $\frac{1}{2}$ ☐ 5%.

1. Change each number to a decimal.

$\frac{1}{2} = .5$

$5\% = .05$

2. Compare the decimals.

$.5 > .05$, so $\frac{1}{2} > 5\%$

Compare. You may want to use the chart on page 94 to help you. Write <, >, or =.

1.

$\frac{2}{5}$ **>** 20%

$\frac{2}{5} = .4$

$20\% = .20$

$.4 > .20$, so $\frac{2}{5} > 20\%$

2. $\frac{1}{8}$ ☐ 12%

3. $\frac{1}{3}$ ☐ $33\frac{1}{3}\%$

4. 10% ☐ $\frac{1}{4}$

5. 95% ☐ $\frac{3}{4}$

6. $1\frac{1}{2}\%$ ☐ $\frac{1}{2}$

7. $\frac{1}{5}$ ☐ 30%

8. 41% ☐ $\frac{7}{10}$

9. $\frac{5}{6}$ ☐ $83\frac{1}{3}\%$

10. 25% ☐ $\frac{1}{4}$

11. $\frac{3}{5}$ ☐ 50%

12. 75% ☐ $\frac{2}{3}$

13. $\frac{1}{6}$ ☐ 20%

14. $33\frac{1}{3}\%$ ☐ $\frac{3}{8}$

15. $\frac{5}{6}$ ☐ 85%

16. $\frac{5}{8}$ ☐ 60%

17. Kai can buy a CD player for $\frac{1}{4}$ off or 20% off. Which is the better offer: $\frac{1}{4}$ off or 20% off?

18. The price of a CD Kai wants is marked down 25% in one store, and $\frac{1}{3}$ off in another store. Which is the better value: 25% off or $\frac{1}{3}$ off?

Answer_____

Answer_____

Problem Solving: Using a Budget

This budget shows the average amount that Creative Cleaners spends each month on equipment, taxes, advertising, telephone expenses, transportation, insurance, and miscellaneous expenses.

$ 2,400	Equipment
3,720	Taxes
600	Miscellaneous
1,200	Advertising
1,440	Telephone
1,800	Transportation
840	Insurance
$12,000	

If you change each amount to a percent, you will find out what part of Creative Cleaners' budget is spent on each item.

Example   Creative Cleaners' budget this month was $12,000. They spent $2,400 on equipment. What percent of their budget did they spend on equipment?

▶ **Step 1.**   Write the amount spent for equipment over the amount of the total budget.

$$\frac{2,400}{12,000}$$

▶ **Step 2.**   Reduce to lowest terms and change the fraction to a percent.

$$\frac{24\cancel{0}\cancel{0}}{120\cancel{0}\cancel{0}} = \frac{24}{120} = \frac{1}{5}$$

$$\frac{1}{5} = .20 = 20\%$$

Creative Cleaners spent 20% of their budget on equipment.

Write a percent for each problem.

1. Creative Cleaners spent $3,720 on taxes. What percent of the budget did they spend on taxes?

2. Creative Cleaners spent $600 on miscellaneous expenses. What percent of the budget did they spend on miscellaneous expenses?

Answer_____

Answer_____

3. Creative Cleaners spent $1,200 on advertising. What percent of the budget did they spend on advertising?

Answer_____

4. Creative Cleaners spent $1,440 on telephone expenses. What percent of the budget did they spend on telephone expenses?

Answer_____

5. What percent of the budget did Creative Cleaners spend on transportation?

Answer_____

6. What percent of the budget did Creative Cleaners spend on insurance?

Answer_____

7. About $720 of the money for telephone expenses was spent to buy a cellular phone. What percent of their budget is this?

Answer_____

8. Creative Cleaners spent $720 for a cellular phone. What percent of their money for telephone expenses is this?

Answer_____

9. Creative Cleaners spent $360 on newspaper ads. What percent of their advertising money is this?

Answer_____

10. Creative Cleaners spent $360 on newspaper ads. What percent of their budget is this?

Answer_____

11. Creative Cleaners spent $1,080 of their transportation expenses on gasoline. What percent of their transportation expenses is this?

Answer_____

12. Creative Cleaners spent $1,080 on gasoline. What percent of their budget is this?

Answer_____

Unit 4 Review

Write a ratio for each problem. Reduce if possible.

1. 4 bedrooms to 3 bathrooms

2. 5 hotdogs and 10 hamburgers

3. 3 chances out of 100

4. 2 quarts of oil for $3

Solve each proportion.

5. $\frac{1}{2} = \frac{n}{6}$

6. $\frac{2}{8} = \frac{1}{n}$

7. $\frac{n}{70} = \frac{1}{10}$

8. $\frac{6}{n} = \frac{3}{4}$

Write each percent using a percent sign.

9. three percent =

10. ninety-nine percent =

11. six and one third percent =

12. one hundred two percent =

Change each percent to a decimal.

13. 45% =

14. 80% =

15. 2% =

16. $33\frac{1}{3}\% =$

17. 240% =

18. $9\frac{1}{2}\% =$

19. .8% =

20. $66\frac{2}{3}\% =$

Change each decimal to a percent.

21. .3 =

22. .09 =

23. .117 =

24. .25 =

25. 1.8 =

26. 1.01 =

27. .6 =

28. .99 =

Change each percent to a fraction.

29. 30% =

30. 9% =

31. 28% =

32. 300% =

33. 75% =

34. $8\frac{1}{3}\% =$

35. $66\frac{2}{3}\% =$

36. 120% =

Change each fraction to a percent.

37.
$$\frac{1}{4} =$$

38.
$$\frac{2}{3} =$$

39.
$$1\frac{1}{2} =$$

40.
$$6\frac{7}{20} =$$

41.
$$\frac{3}{10} =$$

42.
$$\frac{4}{25} =$$

43.
$$7\frac{3}{4} =$$

44.
$$9\frac{1}{3} =$$

Change each fraction to a decimal and a percent.

45.
$$\frac{1}{100} =$$

46.
$$\frac{1}{2} =$$

47.
$$\frac{2}{3} =$$

48.
$$\frac{1}{4} =$$

49.
$$\frac{3}{4} =$$

50.
$$\frac{1}{3} =$$

51.
$$\frac{7}{10} =$$

52.
$$\frac{1}{8} =$$

Compare. Use <, >, or =.

53.
$$10\% \ \square \ \frac{1}{10}$$

54.
$$.5 \ \square \ 5\%$$

55.
$$\frac{3}{4} \ \square \ 40\%$$

56.
$$26\% \ \square \ 3.1$$

Below is a list of the problems in this review and the pages on which the skills are taught. If you missed any problems, turn to the pages listed and practice the skills. Then correct the problems you missed in the Unit Review.

Problems	Pages	Problems	Pages
1-4	75	29-36	91
5-8	76-78	37-44	92-93
9-12	81	45-52	94
13-20	82-84	53-56	95-96
21-28	86		

Unit 5 USING PERCENTS

People use percents all the time. They use them to compute interest on loans and savings accounts, income taxes, sales tax, tips, and pay raises.

In this unit, you will learn how to solve percent problems and how to use percents in some familiar real-life situations.

Getting Ready

You should be familiar with the skills on this page and the next before you begin this unit.

 You may need to change from a percent to a decimal before you work a problem. Remember, percent means hundredths.

Change each percent to a decimal.

1.
$15\% = 15. = .15$

2.
$9\frac{1}{4}\% =$

3.
$7\% =$

4.
$5\% =$

5.
$20\% =$

6.
$33\% =$

7.
$8.3\% =$

8.
$99\% =$

9.
$105\% =$

10.
$65\% =$

11.
$3\frac{1}{2}\% =$

12.
$14.6\% =$

13.
$300\% =$

14.
$16\% =$

15.
$10\% =$

16.
$250\% =$

For review, see Unit 4, pages 82–84.

Getting Ready

Sometimes you'll have to change a percent to a fraction.

Change each percent to a fraction. Reduce if possible.

17.
$$10\% = \frac{10}{100} = \frac{1}{10}$$

18.
$$1\% =$$

19.
$$20\% =$$

20.
$$25\% =$$

21.
$$33\frac{1}{3}\% =$$

22.
$$66\frac{2}{3}\% =$$

23.
$$50\% =$$

24.
$$60\% =$$

25.
$$40\% =$$

26.
$$75\% =$$

27.
$$80\% =$$

28.
$$100\% =$$

For review, see Unit 4, pages 90-91.

 The answers to some percent problems may need to be rounded.

Round each decimal to the nearest hundredth.

29.
$$1.072 = 1.07$$

30.
$$.333 =$$

31.
$$4.625 =$$

32.
$$10.001 =$$

33.
$$4.366 =$$

34.
$$.695 =$$

35.
$$12.361 =$$

36.
$$186.001 =$$

37.
$$20.455 =$$

38.
$$9.929 =$$

39.
$$340.016 =$$

40.
$$829.405 =$$

For review, see Unit 1, page 27.

 Often when you work percent problems, you will need to multiply or divide with decimals.

Solve.

41.
$$1.23 \times .15 =$$

$$\begin{array}{r} 1.23 \\ \times\ .15 \\ \hline 6\ 15 \\ +\ 12\ 3 \\ \hline .18\ 45 \end{array}$$

42.
$$.05 \times 72 =$$

43.
$$84 \times .25 =$$

44.
$$30 \times .1 =$$

45.
$$10 \div .5 =$$

46.
$$84 \div .21 =$$

47.
$$15.4 \div 20 =$$

48.
$$3.6 \div .4 =$$

For review, see Unit 3, pages 52-56, 62-68.

Understanding Percent Problems

There are three pieces to a percent problem: *the part*, *the whole*, and *the percent*.

10% of 250 is 25

part = 25
whole = the total, 250
percent = the number with the % sign, 10%

Use These Steps

Find the part, the whole, and the percent in: **50% of 150 is 75.**

1. Write the part.

part = 75

2. Write the whole.

whole = 150

3. Write the percent.

percent = 50%

Find the part, the whole, and the percent.

1.
40% of 200 is 80
part = 80
whole = 200
percent = 40%

2.
30% of 60 is 18

3.
90% of 50 is 45

4.
100% of 30 is 30

5.
5% of 500 is 25

6.
8% of 1,200 is 96

7.
150% of 100 is 150

8.
200% of 50 is 100

9.
500% of 20 is 100

10.
12.5% of 80 is 10

11.
$33\frac{1}{3}$% of 60 is 20

12.
4.3% of 1,000 is 43

13. 15% off the original price of a $12,000 car is $1,800.

14. A loan for 80% of the $16,000 sticker-price of a truck is $12,800.

Answer＿＿＿＿＿＿＿＿＿＿＿＿＿

Answer＿＿＿＿＿＿＿＿＿＿＿＿＿

Understanding Percent Problems: The Part

Sometimes in a percent problem, one of the three pieces is missing. You can find the missing piece by using the percent triangle. The percent triangle shows how the three pieces are related.

To solve for the part, cover the word *part*. The remaining pieces are connected by a multiplication sign. Multiply the pieces you have to find the part.

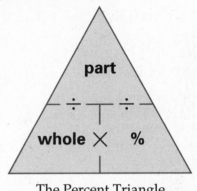

The Percent Triangle

part = whole × percent

Use These Steps

Find the part, the whole, and the percent in: 10% of 250 is what?

1. Write the pieces you have.

   whole = 250
   percent = 10%

2. To find the part, write a percent sentence.

   part = whole × percent

3. Replace the words with the numbers for each piece.

   part = 250 × 10%

Find the part, the whole, and the percent.

1.
65% of 40 is what?
whole = 40
percent = 65%
part = 40 × 65%

2.
32% of 19 is what?

3.
6% of 10 is what?

4.
1% of 327 is what?

5.
250% of 700 is what?

6.
$1\frac{1}{2}$% of 36 is what?

7.
What is 50% of 80?
whole = 80
percent = 50%
part = 80 × 50%

8.
What is $33\frac{1}{3}$% of 9?

9.
What is 125% of 86?

10.
What is 10% of 65?

11.
What is $33\frac{1}{3}$% of 500?

12.
What is 75% of 350?

Understanding Percent Problems: The Whole

In a percent problem, the missing piece may be the whole. Use the percent triangle the same way you did to find the part.

To solve for the whole, cover the word *whole*. The remaining pieces are connected by a division sign. Divide the pieces you have to find the whole.

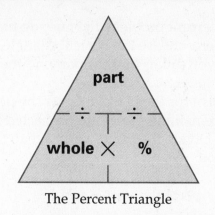

The Percent Triangle

$$whole = part \div percent$$

Use These Steps

Find the part, the whole, and the percent in: 24 is 30% of what number?

1. Write the pieces you have.

    part = 24
    percent = 30%

2. To find the whole, write a percent sentence.

    whole = part ÷ percent

3. Replace the words with the numbers for each piece.

    whole = 24 ÷ 30%

Find the part, the whole, and the percent.

1.
3 is 10% of what number?
part = 3
percent = 10%
whole = 3 ÷ 10%

2.
10 is 25% of what number?

3.
24 is 3% of what number?

4.
15 is 5% of what number?

5.
33 is 110% of what number?

6.
40 is $66\frac{2}{3}$% of what number?

7.
20 is 25% of what number?

8.
7 is 10% of what number?

9.
400 is 200% of what number?

10.
75 is $33\frac{1}{3}$% of what number?

11.
90 is 25% of what number?

12.
130 is 160% of what number?

Understanding Percent Problems: The Percent

In a percent problem, the missing piece may be the percent. Use the percent triangle the same way you did to find the part and the whole.

To solve for the percent, cover the percent sign. The remaining pieces are connected by a division sign. Divide the pieces you have to find the percent.

$$percent = part \div whole$$

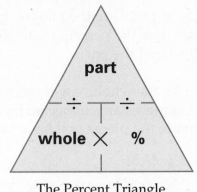

The Percent Triangle

Use These Steps

Find the part, the whole, and the percent in: **What percent of 40 is 20?**

1. Write the pieces you have.

    part = 20
    whole = 40

2. To find the percent, write a percent sentence.

    percent = part ÷ whole

3. Replace the words with the numbers for each piece.

    percent = 20 ÷ 40

Find the part, the whole, and the percent.

1.
What percent of 16 is 4?
part = 4
whole = 16
percent = 4 ÷ 16

2.
What percent of 20 is 10?

3.
What percent of 120 is 4?

4.
What percent of 100 is 1?

5.
What percent of 36 is 72?

6.
What percent of 4 is 8?

7.
10 is what percent of 12?
part = 10
whole = 12
percent = 10 ÷ 12

8.
3 is what percent of 2?

9.
75 is what percent of 25?

10.
12 is what percent of 3?

11.
150 is what percent of 200?

12.
15 is what percent of 25?

Finding the Part: Changing Percents to Decimals

Remember, you can find the part in a percent problem by using this sentence:

$$\text{part} = \text{whole} \times \text{percent}$$

Change the percent to a decimal. Then multiply to find the part.

Use These Steps

What is 15% of 900?

1. Write the pieces.

   whole = 900
   percent = 15%
   part = 900 × 15%

2. Change the percent to a decimal.

   15% = 15. = .15

3. Multiply 900 by .15 to find the part.

   900 × .15 = 135

Find the part.

1.
What is 10% of 20?
whole = 20
percent = 10% = .1
part = 20 × .1 = 2

2.
What is 95% of 300?

3.
What is 5% of 60?

4.
What is 22% of 50?

5.
What is 36% of 125?

6.
What is 60% of 250?

7.
15% of 280 is what?
whole = 280
percent = 15% = .15
part = 280 × .15 = 42

8.
12% of 300 is what?

9.
5% of 80 is what?

10. Mr. Richards pays 15% for federal taxes. He earns $1,000 each month. How much federal tax does he pay each month?

11. Mr. Richards pays a state tax of 4% on the money he earns. How much did he pay for state taxes?

Answer _____

Answer _____

Finding the Part: Changing Complex Percents to Decimals

In some problems, the percent you're working with may be a complex percent. To solve the problem, change the percent to a decimal.

Use These Steps

What is $1\frac{1}{2}\%$ of 400?

1. Write the pieces.

whole = 400

percent = $1\frac{1}{2}\%$

part = $400 \times 1\frac{1}{2}\%$

2. Change the percent to a decimal.

$1\frac{1}{2}\% = 1.5\% = 01.5 = .015$

3. Multiply 400 by .015 to find the part.

$400 \times .015 = 6$

Find the part.

1.

What is $8\frac{1}{5}\%$ of 500?

whole = 500

percent = $8\frac{1}{5}\% = .082$

part = $500 \times .082 = 41$

2.

What is $16\frac{1}{2}\%$ of 400?

3.

What is $24\frac{1}{4}\%$ of 400?

4.

What is $60\frac{3}{4}\%$ of 800?

5.

What is $4\frac{2}{5}\%$ of 250?

6.

What is $7\frac{3}{10}\%$ of 1,000?

7.

$62\frac{1}{2}\%$ of 480 is what?

whole = 480

percent = $62\frac{1}{2}\% = .625$

part = $480 \times .625 = 300$

8.

$7\frac{3}{5}\%$ of 500 is what?

9.

$12\frac{1}{2}\%$ of 24 is what?

10.

$9\frac{4}{5}\%$ of 1,500 is what?

Finding the Part: Changing Percents to Fractions

When solving for the part, it may be easier to change the percent to a fraction instead of to a decimal. Remember, a percent can be changed to a fraction by dropping the percent sign and writing the percent as the numerator of a fraction with 100 as the denominator.

The table on page 94 lists some common percents and fractions.

Use These Steps

Find the three pieces in: What is 50% of 24?

1. Write the pieces.

   whole = 24
   percent = 50%
   part = 24 × 50%

2. Change the percent to a fraction. Reduce.

   $50\% = \dfrac{50}{100} = \dfrac{1}{2}$

3. Multiply 24 by $\dfrac{1}{2}$ to find the part.

   $\dfrac{\overset{12}{\cancel{24}}}{1} \times \dfrac{1}{\underset{1}{\cancel{2}}} = \dfrac{12}{1} = 12$

Find the part.

1.
What is 30% of 20?
whole = 20
percent = 30% = $\dfrac{3\cancel{0}}{10\cancel{0}} = \dfrac{3}{10}$

part = $\dfrac{\overset{2}{\cancel{20}}}{1} \times \dfrac{3}{\underset{1}{\cancel{10}}} = \dfrac{6}{1} = 6$

2.
What is 25% of 32?

3.
What is 15% of 240?

4.
10% of 500 is what?
whole = 500
percent = 10% = $\dfrac{1\cancel{0}}{10\cancel{0}} = \dfrac{1}{10}$

part = $\dfrac{\overset{50}{\cancel{500}}}{1} \times \dfrac{1}{\underset{1}{\cancel{10}}} = \dfrac{50}{1} = 50$

5.
50% of 80 is what?

6.
20% of 125 is what?

7. Combined, members of the cycling club spent $250 one month on bike repairs. They spent 24% of the amount repairing bike chains. How much money did they spend repairing bike chains?

8. The cycling club spent 60% of the $250 repairing tires. How much money did they spend on tire repair?

Answer _____

Answer _____

Finding the Part: Changing Complex Percents to Fractions

When you solve problems that use percents such as $33\frac{1}{3}\%$ and $66\frac{2}{3}\%$ that don't have an exact decimal equivalent, use their fraction equivalent. You may want to use the table on page 94 to find some of the common fraction equivalents.

Use These Steps

What is $33\frac{1}{3}\%$ of 24?

1. Write the pieces.

   whole = 24
   percent = $33\frac{1}{3}\%$
   part = $24 \times 33\frac{1}{3}\%$

2. Change the percent to a fraction.

   $33\frac{1}{3}\% = \frac{1}{3}$

3. Multiply 24 by $\frac{1}{3}$ to find the part.

   $\overset{8}{\cancel{\frac{24}{1}}} \times \frac{1}{\underset{1}{\cancel{3}}} = \frac{8}{1} = 8$

Find the part.

1.
   What is $66\frac{2}{3}\%$ of 90?
   whole = 90
   percent = $66\frac{2}{3}\% = \frac{2}{3}$
   part = $\overset{30}{\cancel{\frac{90}{1}}} \times \frac{2}{\underset{1}{\cancel{3}}} = \frac{60}{1} = 60$

2.
   What is $83\frac{1}{3}\%$ of 66?

3.
   What is $16\frac{2}{3}\%$ of 180?

4.
   What is $83\frac{1}{3}\%$ of 216?

5.
   What is $16\frac{2}{3}\%$ of 42?

6.
   What is $33\frac{1}{3}\%$ of 720?

7. A veterinarian gave 99 shots. She gave $66\frac{2}{3}\%$ of the shots to dogs. How many shots did she give to dogs?

8. She gave $33\frac{1}{3}\%$ of the shots to cats. How many shots did she give to cats?

Answer_____   Answer_____

Finding the Part: Percents Greater than 100%

Sometimes the percent you're looking for will be greater than 100%. To solve the problem, you can change the percent to a decimal or to a fraction, whichever is easier. Remember, if you have 100% of something, you have the whole thing.

Use These Steps

What is 110% of 50?

1. Write the pieces.

    whole = 50
    percent = 110%
    part = 50 × 110%

2. Change the percent to a decimal or to an improper fraction. Reduce.

    $110\% = 110. = 1.10 = 1.1$

    or

    $110\% = \frac{110}{100} = \frac{11}{10}$

3. Multiply 50 by 1.1 or by $\frac{11}{10}$ to find the part.

    $50 \times 1.1 = 55.0 = 55$

    or

    $50 \times \frac{11}{10} = \frac{50}{1} \times \frac{11}{10} = \frac{55}{1} = 55$

Find the part.

1. What is 250% of 90?
    whole = 90
    percent = 250% = 2.50 or $\frac{5}{2}$
    part = 90 × 2.5 = 225
    or
    $90 \times \frac{5}{2} = \frac{90}{1} \times \frac{5}{2} = \frac{225}{1} = 225$

2. What is 130% of 10?

3. What is 325% of 100?

4. What is 500% of 75?

5. What is 110% of 500?

6. What is 450% of 780?

7. What is 725% of 60?

8. What is 900% of 15?

Mixed Review

Find the part.

1.

What is 32% of 75?

2.

What is 25% of 20?

3.

What is 10% of 120?

4.

What is 50% of 48?

5.

What is $12\frac{1}{2}$% of 80?

6.

What is $33\frac{1}{3}$% of 6?

7.

What is $6\frac{1}{4}$% of 400?

8.

What is $14\frac{1}{2}$% of 200?

9.

What is $5\frac{3}{4}$% of 400?

10.

What is 10% of 900?

11.

What is 400% of 29?

12.

What is 105% of 700?

13. Mr. Brent bought car insurance from Everystate Insurance Company. The total bill was $400. He made a down payment of 20% of the total bill. How much was Mr. Brent's down payment?

14. 95% of the students who enter Lincoln High School will graduate. If 320 students enter the school next year, how many will graduate?

Answer _____

Answer _____

Problem Solving: Using an Interest Formula

People earn interest on money they keep in a savings account. They pay interest on a loan. You can compute simple interest by using the following formula. A formula uses letters which can be replaced with numbers.

The simple interest formula is   I = prt

I = interest
p = principal—the amount borrowed or saved
r = rate—the percent charged each year
    (annually) for loans or earned on savings
t = time in years

I = prt tells you that you find the amount of interest by multiplying the principal by the rate by the time.

Example Mr. Garrett borrowed $600 from the bank. The bank charged $9\frac{1}{2}\%$ annual interest. Mr. Garrett paid back the money in 1 year. How much interest did he pay?

▶ **Step 1.** Write the formula. Substitute the given information for each letter.

$$I = prt$$
$$I = \$600 \times 9\tfrac{1}{2}\% \times 1$$

▶ **Step 2.** Change the percent to a decimal. Multiply to find the answer.

$$I = \$600 \times .095 \times 1 = \$57.000$$
$57.000 rounds to $57.00

Mr. Garrett paid $57.00 in interest.

Solve. Round to the nearest hundredth, or cent.

1. Mrs. Sand borrowed $600 for 1 year. The bank charged $8\frac{1}{2}\%$ annual interest. How much did Mrs. Sand pay in interest?

2. Mr. Evans borrowed $2,000 for 1 year. The bank charged $10\frac{3}{4}\%$ annual interest. How much did Mr. Evans pay in interest?

Answer _____

Answer _____

Solve. Round to the nearest hundredth, or cent.

3. Nancy's aunt borrowed $900 from her credit union for 2 years. The annual interest rate for the loan was 7%. How much did she pay in interest charges?

Answer_____

4. Brian is planning to borrow $2,500 to buy a car. He will pay 6% annual interest and pay back the loan in $2\frac{1}{2}$ years. How much interest will he pay?

Answer_____

5. Lolita kept $200 in her savings account for a year. The bank pays $6\frac{1}{2}$% interest per year. How much interest did she receive at the end of 1 year?

Answer_____

6. Lee deposited $275 in his savings account 2 years ago. He earns 4% interest annually. How much interest has he earned?

Answer_____

7. Ms. Francis inherited $2,000. She put the money into an account paying $7\frac{1}{4}$% annual interest. How much interest did she receive in 1 year?

Answer_____

8. At the beginning of the year, Fern's dad deposited $800 in a savings account paying $6\frac{1}{4}$% annual interest. How much interest did he earn in 1 year?

Answer_____

9. Jesse's savings account earns $6\frac{3}{4}$% annual interest. If he deposits $400 in his account, how much interest will he receive at the end of 1 year?

Answer_____

10. Bonita had $100 in a savings account paying 5% annual interest. How much interest will she receive at the end of the first year?

Answer_____

Finding the Part: Using a Proportion

You can also solve percent problems by using a proportion. Since percent means hundredths, you can use the following proportion to find the missing number.

$$\frac{\text{part}}{\text{whole}} = \frac{\%}{100}$$

Use n to stand for the part. Cross-multiply to find n, the part.

Use These Steps

What is 3% of 300?

1. Write a proportion.

$$\frac{n}{300} = \frac{3}{100}$$

2. Cross-multiply to find n, the part.

$$\frac{n}{300} \times \frac{3}{100}$$
$$100 \times n = 3 \times 300$$
$$100\,n = 900$$
$$n = 900 \div 100 = 9$$

Write a proportion for each problem. Cross-multiply to find the part.

1. What is 30% of 40?

$$\frac{n}{40} \times \frac{30}{100}$$
$$100 \times n = 30 \times 40$$
$$100\,n = 1,200$$
$$n = 1,200 \div 100 = 12$$

2. What is 10% of 90?

3. What is 25% of 32?

4. What is 75% of 80?

5. What is 85% of 100?

6. What is 50% of 10?

7. 52% of the seniors at South High School participate in sports. How many of the 125 seniors participate in sports?

8. Maxine saves 15% of her allowance each week. If her allowance is $20 each week, how much does she save?

Answer_____

Answer_____

Finding the Part: Using a Proportion

When cross-multiplying, remember to multiply n by the number in the opposite corner first.

Use These Steps

What is 10% of 12?

1. Write a proportion.

$$\frac{n}{20} = \frac{10}{100}$$

2. Cross-multiply to find n, the part. Write the answer as a decimal.

$$\frac{n}{20} \bowtie \frac{10}{100}$$
$$100 \times n = 10 \times 20$$
$$100\,n = 200$$
$$n = 200 \div 100 = 2$$

Write a proportion. Solve for the part.

1.
What is 30% of 120?
$$\frac{n}{120} \bowtie \frac{30}{100}$$
$$100 \times n = 30 \times 120$$
$$100\,n = 3{,}600$$
$$n = 3{,}600 \div 100 = 36$$

2. What is 50% of 50?

3. What is 25% of 60?

4. What is 95% of 520?

5. What is 5% of 40?

6. What is 2% of 100?

7. What is 10% of 750?

8. What is 20% of 300?

9. What is 15% of 240?

Problem Solving: Using Percents

When prices go up by a certain percent, you can figure out what the new price will be. The new price will be 100% of the old price plus a percent of the old price.

Example The price of a truck has increased by 10%. If the old price was $6,590, what is the new price?

Step 1. The new price is 100% of the old price plus 10% of the old price.

$$100\% + 10\% = 110\%$$

Step 2. Write a proportion. Cross-multiply.

$$\frac{n}{\$6,590} \diagtimes \frac{110}{100}$$
$$n \times 100 = \$6,590 \times 110$$
$$100\,n = \$724,900$$
$$n = \$724,900 \div 100 = \$7,249$$

The new price is $7,249.

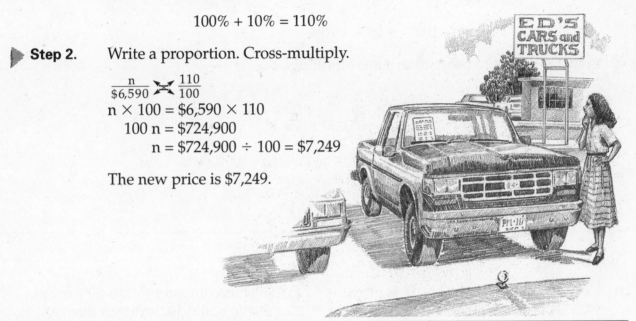

Solve.

1. Last year Peter made $3,000 working at a restaurant. This year he received a 5% raise. How much will he make this year?

Answer_____

2. Last year the restaurant employed 40 people. This year they have 20% more people working for them. How many people now work at the restaurant?

Answer_____

3. Steve has 60 CDs. He plans to increase his collection by 15%. How many CDs will he have then?

Answer_____

4. Before its last tune-up, Hal's truck went 15 miles on a gallon of gas. After the tune-up it went 20% farther. How many miles per gallon did the truck get after the tune-up?

Answer_____

When prices go down by a certain percent, you can figure out the new price. The new price will be 100% of the old price minus a percent of the old price.

Example The local used car dealership is having a 25% off clearance sale on certain cars. If a car used to cost $5,000, what is the new price?

▶ **Step 1.** The new price is 100% of the old price minus 25% of the old price.

$$100\% - 25\% = 75\%$$

▶ **Step 2.** Write a proportion. Cross-multiply.

$$\frac{n}{\$5,000} \quad \frac{75}{100}$$
$$n \times 100 = \$5,000 \times 75$$
$$100\,n = \$375,000$$
$$n = \$375,000 \div 100 = \$3,750$$

The new price is $3,750.

Solve.

1. Last year the price of a bus ticket was $4. This year the price decreased by 25%. What is the new price?

Answer_____

2. The bus company thinks 20% fewer people will ride the buses this year. If 24,250 people rode the buses last year, how many people will ride the buses this year?

Answer_____

3. Last summer Athena babysat 40 hours per week. This summer she will babysit 30% fewer hours. How many hours per week will she babysit?

Answer_____

4. Last summer Athena's take-home pay was $280 per week. This summer she will be taking home 25% less money. What will her weekly pay be?

Answer_____

Finding the Part: Using a Proportion With Complex Percents

To use a proportion to solve problems with complex percents, use the fraction equivalent for the percent. Then cross-multiply.

You can refer to the table on page 94 for some common percents and their fraction equivalents.

Use These Steps

What is $33\frac{1}{3}$% of 150?

1. Write a proportion. Write $33\frac{1}{3}$% as $\frac{1}{3}$.

$$\frac{n}{150} = \frac{1}{3}$$

2. Cross-multiply to find n, the part.

$$\frac{n}{150} \diagup\!\!\!\!\diagdown \frac{1}{3}$$
$$n \times 3 = 150 \times 1$$
$$3\,n = 150$$
$$n = 150 \div 3 = 50$$

Use the table on page 94 to find the equivalent fractions. Write a proportion. Find the part.

1.
What is $66\frac{2}{3}$% of 90?
$$\frac{n}{90} \diagup\!\!\!\!\diagdown \frac{2}{3}$$
$$n \times 3 = 90 \times 2$$
$$3\,n = 180$$
$$n = 180 \div 3 = 60$$

2.
What is $12\frac{1}{2}$% of 16?

3.
What is $62\frac{1}{2}$% of 32?

4.
What is $16\frac{2}{3}$% of 6?

5.
What is $37\frac{1}{2}$% of 64?

6.
What is $83\frac{1}{3}$% of 240?

7. Associated Electronics offers employees a $33\frac{1}{3}$% discount on all purchases. How much would an employee save on a $450 air conditioner?

8. $37\frac{1}{2}$% of the 88 seniors at Union High School participate in winter sports. How many of the seniors are involved in winter sports?

Answer_____

Answer_____

Application

When you figure the amount of sales tax you pay or the amount you save at a sale, you are finding the part.

Example The sales tax in Johnson City is 7%. What is the sales tax on a $200 sofa sold in Johnson City?

Using a Percent Sentence:

part (tax) = whole (cost) × percent (tax rate)

part = $200 × 7%

part = $200 × .07 = $14

The sales tax is $14.

Using a Proportion:

$$\frac{n}{\$200} \bowtie \frac{7}{100}$$

n × 100 = $200 × 7

100 n = $1,400

n = $1,400 ÷ 100 = $14

Solve. Use either a percent sentence or a proportion.

1. Mary's Clothing Mart is reducing all merchandise by 25%. By how much will a $40 dress be marked down?

    Answer_____

2. Book Barn sells books at $33\frac{1}{3}$% off the regular price. If a book usually sells for $30, by how much will the manager of Book Barn mark it down?

    Answer_____

3. Place Appliance is offering a discount of 40% on a discontinued washing machine. If the washer normally costs $350, how much is the discount?

    Answer_____

4. Mr. Allen spent 10% of his monthly pay on a new television. He earned $1,520 in April. How much did he spend on the television set?

    Answer_____

5. Last year the price of a Handy home computer was $1,200. This year the price decreased 32%. How much less does the computer cost this year?

    Answer_____

6. The sales tax in Landsburg is 8%. How much sales tax did John pay on a new guitar that cost $450?

    Answer_____

Mixed Review

Find the part using a proportion.

1. What is 20% of 40?

2. What is 50% of 90?

3. What is 37% of 100?

4. What is 60% of 340?

5. What is 4% of 50?

6. What is 1% of 500?

7. What is $33\frac{1}{3}$% of 126?

8. What is $12\frac{1}{2}$% of 256?

9. What is $16\frac{2}{3}$% of 90?

10. What is $66\frac{2}{3}$% of 72?

11. What is 300% of 10?

12. What is 130% of 280?

13. Cora put $85 worth of clothing on layaway. She had to make a 20% down payment. How much was Cora's down payment?

14. Thriftee Cleaners gives a 15% discount on cleaning orders over twenty dollars. Mrs. Kim's total order was $40. How much did she save?

Answer_____

Answer_____

Finding the Whole: Changing Percents to Decimals

You can find the whole in a percent problem by using this sentence:

whole = part ÷ percent

Change the percent to a decimal. Then divide.

Use These Steps

22 is 10% of what number?

1. Write the pieces.

part = 22
percent = 10%
whole = 22 ÷ 10%

2. Change the percent to a decimal.

10% = .1

3. Divide 22 by .1 to find the whole.

22 ÷ .1 = 220

Find the whole.

1.
38 is 20% of what number?
part = 38
percent = 20% = .2
whole = 38 ÷ .2 = 190

2.
50 is 200% of what number?

3.
7 is 5% of what number?

4.
15 is 3% of what number?

5.
12 is 50% of what number?

6.
90 is 45% of what number?

7.
120 is 60% of what number?

8.
420 is 70% of what number?

Finding the Whole: Changing Complex Percents

In some problems, the percent may be a complex percent. To solve the problem, change the percent to a decimal.

Use These Steps

11 is $5\frac{1}{2}$% of what number?

1. Write the pieces.

part = 20
percent = $5\frac{1}{2}$%
whole = 11 ÷ $5\frac{1}{2}$%

2. Change the percent to a decimal.

$5\frac{1}{2}$% = 5.5% = .055

3. Divide 11 by .055 to find the whole.

11 ÷ .055 = 200

Solve for the part.

1.
36 is $37\frac{1}{2}$% of what number?
part = 36
percent = $37\frac{1}{2}$% = .375
whole = 36 ÷ .375 = 96

2.
45 is $62\frac{1}{2}$% of what number?

3.
97 is $24\frac{1}{4}$% of what number?

4.
594 is $6\frac{3}{4}$% of what number?

5.
22 is $4\frac{2}{5}$% of what number?

6.
3 is $1\frac{1}{2}$% of what number?

7.
4 is $12\frac{1}{2}$% of what number?

8.
21 is $5\frac{1}{4}$% of what number?

9.
175 is $87\frac{1}{2}$% of what number?

10.
17 is $8\frac{1}{2}$% of what number?

Finding the Whole: Changing Percents to Fractions

Sometimes it is easier to change the percent to a fraction instead of to a decimal. Remember, when you divide by a fraction, invert the fraction and then multiply. Use the table on page 94 to help you.

Use These Steps

50 is 25% of what number?

1. Write the pieces.

    part = 50
    percent = 25%
    whole = 50 ÷ 25%

2. Change the percent to a fraction. Reduce if possible.

    $25\% = \frac{25}{100} = \frac{1}{4}$

3. Divide 50 by $\frac{1}{4}$ to find the whole.

    $\frac{50}{1} \div \frac{1}{4} = \frac{50}{1} \times \frac{4}{1} = \frac{200}{1} = 200$

Find the whole.

1.
   70 is 50% of what number?
   part = 70

   percent = 50% = $\frac{50}{100}$ = $\frac{1}{2}$

   whole = $\frac{70}{1}$ ÷ $\frac{1}{2}$ = $\frac{70}{1}$ × $\frac{2}{1}$ = $\frac{140}{1}$ = 140

2.
   32 is 20% of what number?

3.
   20 is 250% of what number?

4.
   10 is 40% of what number?

5.
   4 is 10% of what number?

6.
   88 is 22% of what number?

7. 75% of the registered voters in Met County voted in April. If 1,500 people voted, how many registered voters are there in Met County?

8. 20% of the units in Hill Apartments are two-bedroom units. If 12 units have two bedrooms, how many units are there in the whole apartment complex?

Answer_____

Answer_____

Finding the Whole: Complex Percents

Some problems use complex percents such as $33\frac{1}{3}\%$ and $66\frac{2}{3}\%$. When this happens, change the percent to a fraction instead of to a decimal. Then invert and multiply. You may want to use the table on page 94 to help you.

Use These Steps

50 is $66\frac{2}{3}\%$ of what number?

1. Write the pieces.

part = 50
percent = $66\frac{2}{3}\%$
whole = $50 \div 66\frac{2}{3}\%$

2. Change the percent to a fraction.

$$66\frac{2}{3}\% = \frac{2}{3}$$

3. Divide 50 by $\frac{2}{3}$ to find the whole.

$$\frac{50}{1} \div \frac{2}{3} = \frac{\overset{25}{\cancel{50}}}{1} \times \frac{3}{\underset{1}{\cancel{2}}} = \frac{75}{1} = 75$$

Find the whole.

1.
18 is $12\frac{1}{2}\%$ of what number?

part = 18

percent = $12\frac{1}{2}\% = \frac{1}{8}$

whole = $\frac{18}{1} \div \frac{1}{8} = \frac{18}{1} \times \frac{8}{1} = \frac{144}{1} = 144$

2. 25 is $62\frac{1}{2}\%$ of what number?

3. 95 is $33\frac{1}{3}\%$ of what number?

4. 102 is $16\frac{2}{3}\%$ of what number?

5. 8 is $66\frac{2}{3}\%$ of what number?

6. 12 is $37\frac{1}{2}\%$ of what number?

7. 8 is $16\frac{2}{3}\%$ of what number?

8. 15 is $83\frac{1}{3}\%$ of what number?

9. 320 is $66\frac{2}{3}\%$ of what number?

10. 25 is $33\frac{1}{3}\%$ of what number?

Mixed Review

Find the missing piece.

1.

What is 50% of 10?

2.

16 is 20% of what number?

3.

What is 1% of 250?

4.

What is 30% of 90?

5.

25 is $33\frac{1}{3}$% of what number?

6.

90 is 300% of what number?

7.

What is 150% of 40?

8.

2 is 10% of what number?

9.

16 is 8% of what number?

10.

10 is 5% of what number?

11.

What is $12\frac{1}{2}$% of 160?

12.

What is 17% of 600?

Finding the Whole: Using a Proportion

When the missing number is the whole, you can find it by using a proportion. Use the proportion:

$$\frac{\text{part}}{\text{whole}} = \frac{\%}{100}$$

Use These Steps

6 is 5% of what number?

1. Write a proportion.

$$\frac{6}{n} = \frac{5}{100}$$

2. Cross-multiply to find n, the whole.

$$\frac{6}{n} \times \frac{5}{100}$$

$n \times 5 = 6 \times 100$

$5\,n = 600$

$n = 600 \div 5 = 120$

Write a proportion for each problem. Cross-multiply to find the whole.

1.

10 is 40% of what number?

$$\frac{10}{n} \times \frac{40}{100}$$

$n \times 40 = 10 \times 100$

$40\,n = 1,000$

$n = 1,000 \div 40 = 25$

2.

39 is 1% of what number?

3.

80 is 10% of what number?

4.

66 is 120% of what number?

5.

30 is 75% of what number?

6.

47 is 5% of what number?

Finding the Whole: Using a Proportion

In problems with complex percents, change the percent to an equivalent fraction. Then cross-multiply to find the missing number.

Use These Steps

18 is $33\frac{1}{3}\%$ of what number?

1. Write a proportion. Write $33\frac{1}{3}\%$ as $\frac{1}{3}$.

$$\frac{18}{n} = \frac{1}{3}$$

2. Cross-multiply to find n, the whole.

$$\frac{18}{n} \bowtie \frac{1}{3}$$
$$1 \times n = 18 \times 3$$
$$n = 54$$

Write a proportion for each problem. Cross-multiply to find the whole.

1.
20 is $66\frac{2}{3}\%$ of what number?

$$\frac{20}{n} \bowtie \frac{2}{3}$$
$$n \times 2 = 20 \times 3$$
$$2n = 60$$
$$n = 60 \div 2 = 30$$

2.
6 is $12\frac{1}{2}\%$ of what number?

3.
45 is $83\frac{1}{3}\%$ of what number?

4.
2 is $16\frac{2}{3}\%$ of what number?

5.
87 is $37\frac{1}{2}\%$ of what number?

6.
110 is $33\frac{1}{3}\%$ of what number?

7.
48 is $66\frac{2}{3}\%$ of what number?

8.
30 is $62\frac{1}{2}\%$ of what number?

Application

In many situations, you know the percent and the part, and you need to find the original amount.

Example Mark's Resale Shop is having a 25%-off sale. If Mr. Jones marks down a winter coat by $10, what was the original cost of the coat?

$$\frac{\text{part (savings)}}{\text{whole (original cost)}} = \frac{\text{percent (sale \%)}}{100}$$

$$\frac{\$10}{n} \bowtie \frac{25}{100}$$

$$n \times 25 = \$10 \times 100$$
$$25\,n = \$1,000$$
$$n = \$1,000 \div 25 = \$40$$

The coat originally cost $40.

Solve.

1. Value World sells radios at a 20% discount. What was the original cost of a radio marked by the manager as $4 off?

   Answer_____

2. Collier's Music Store is offering a 10% discount on the cost of a drum set. If Mr. Collier makes a sign that says "Save $35," what was the original cost?

   Answer_____

3. Lisa's aunt saves 15% of her monthly pay. She saved $150 last month. How much does Lisa's aunt make a month?

   Answer_____

4. Ms. Thomas gives customers a 25% discount if they get their hair cut before 10 A.M. A customer saved $7. How much would she have paid after 10 A.M.?

   Answer_____

5. A car dealer is offering a rebate of $600. The dealer says that this amount is 10% of the price of a certain car. How much is the car?

   Answer_____

6. In the Southwest Mall, 75% of the stores are open for business. Cathy counted 30 open stores. How many stores are there in the mall?

   Answer_____

Mixed Review

Solve each problem using a proportion.

1. 15 is 10% of what number?

2. What is 30% of 200?

3. What is 20% of 45?

4. 87 is 25% of what number?

5. 44 is 110% of what number?

6. What is 95% of 80?

7. What is 50% of 10?

8. 6 is 75% of what number?

9. 10 is $33\frac{1}{3}$% of what number?

10. What is $87\frac{1}{2}$% of 16?

11. What is $66\frac{2}{3}$% of 12?

12. 3 is 15% of what number?

Finding the Percent

You can find the percent in a percent problem by using this percent sentence:

$$\text{percent} = \text{part} \div \text{whole}$$

Use These Steps

30 is what percent of 120?

1. Write the pieces.

part = 30
whole = 120
percent = 30 ÷ 120

2. Divide 30 by 120.

30 ÷ 120 = .25

3. Change .25 to a percent.

.25 = 25%

Find the percent.

1.
10 is what percent of 20?
part = 10
whole = 20
percent = 10 ÷ 20 = .5 = 50%

2.
27 is what percent of 108?

3.
8 is what percent of 40?

4.
60 is what percent of 600?

5.
93 is what percent of 100?

6.
146 is what percent of 2,920?

7.
340 is what percent of 400?

8.
120 is what percent of 300?

9.
430 is what percent of 500?

10.
110 is what percent of 250?

Finding the Percent

When finding the percent, you can write the percent as a decimal or as its fraction equivalent.

Use These Steps

15 is what percent of 1,000?

1. Write the pieces.

    part = 15
    whole = 1,000
    percent = 15 ÷ 1,000

2. Divide 15 by 1,000.

    15 ÷ 1,000 = .015

3. Change .015 to a percent.

    $.015 = 1.5\%$ or $1\frac{1}{2}\%$

Find the percent.

1.

8 is what percent of 320?
part = 8
whole = 320
percent = $8 ÷ 320 = .025 = 2.5\%$ or $2\frac{1}{2}\%$

2.

10 is what percent of 400?

3.

19 is what percent of 500?

4.

30 is what percent of 800?

5.

75 is what percent of 6,000?

6.

84 is what percent of 960?

7.

6 is what percent of 250?

8.

50 is what percent of 2,000?

9.

24 is what percent of 64?

10.

400 is what percent of 640?

11.

210 is what percent of 240?

12.

189 is what percent of 1,500?

Finding the Percent

In some problems, the answer will be a complex percent.

Use These Steps

25 is what percent of 75?

1. Write the pieces.

   part = 25
   whole = 75
   percent = 25 ÷ 75

2. Divide 25 by 75.

   $25 \div 75 = .33\frac{1}{3}$

3. Change $.33\frac{1}{3}$ to a percent.

   $.33\frac{1}{3} = 33\frac{1}{3}\%$

Find the percent.

1.
   20 is what percent of 60?
   part = 20
   whole = 60
   percent = $20 \div 60 = 33\frac{1}{3} = 33\frac{1}{3}\%$

2. 14 is what percent of 21?

3. 5 is what percent of 60?

4. 16 is what percent of 24?

5. 11 is what percent of 66?

6. 85 is what percent of 102?

7. 22 is what percent of 66?

8. 96 is what percent of 144?

9. 75 is what percent of 90?

10. 12 is what percent of 72?

Mixed Review

Find the percent.

1.

4 is what percent of 8?

2.

22 is what percent of 88?

3.

9 is what percent of 120?

4.

15 is what percent of 200?

5.

38 is what percent of 228?

6.

40 is what percent of 60?

7.

93 is what percent of 100?

8.

2 is what percent of 50?

9.

125 is what percent of 625?

10.

50 is what percent of 5,000?

11.

70 is what percent of 280?

12.

85 is what percent of 136?

13.

31 is what percent of 93?

14.

65 is what percent of 78?

Finding the Percent: Using a Proportion

You can use a proportion to find the percent. Use the proportion:

$$\frac{\text{part}}{\text{whole}} = \frac{\%}{100}$$

Substitute the correct numbers in the proportion and cross-multiply to find the percent.

Notice when you use a proportion, you write a percent sign after the answer.

Use These Steps

5 is what percent of 25?

1. Write the proportion.

$$\frac{5}{25} = \frac{n}{100}$$

2. Cross-multiply to find n. Add a percent sign.

$$\frac{5}{25} \bowtie \frac{n}{100}$$
$$25 \times n = 5 \times 100$$
$$25\,n = 500$$
$$n = 500 \div 25 = 20 = 20\%$$

Write a proportion for each problem. Cross-multiply to find the percent.

1.

10 is what percent of 200?

$$\frac{10}{200} \bowtie \frac{n}{100}$$
$$200 \times n = 10 \times 100$$
$$200\,n = 1{,}000$$
$$n = 1{,}000 \div 200 = 5 = 5\%$$

2.

8 is what percent of 64?

3.

15 is what percent of 45?

4.

33 is what percent of 55?

5.

70 is what percent of 100?

6.

63 is what percent of 420?

Percent of Increase

When prices increase, people often want to know what percent this increase represents. To find the percent, subtract the old price from the new price. Divide the answer by the old price. Change the answer to a percent.

Use These Steps

What is the percent of increase from $3 to $4?

1. Subtract the old price from the new price to find the change in price.

$$\$4 - \$3 = \$1$$

2. Divide the change in price by the old price.

$$\$1 \div \$3 = .33\frac{1}{3}$$

3. Change to a percent.

$$.33\frac{1}{3} = 33\frac{1}{3}\%$$

Find the percent of increase.

	old price	new price	change in price	% of increase
1.	$ 2	$ 3	$3 − $2 = $1	$1 ÷ $2 = .5 = 50%
2.	$ 8	$ 10		
3.	$ 10	$ 13		
4.	$ 20	$ 22		
5.	$ 32	$ 40		
6.	$ 36	$ 72		
7.	$ 80	$100		
8.	$150	$175		

Percent of Decrease

Sometimes the prices on some items go down. To find the percent of decrease, subtract the new price from the old price. Then divide by the old price. Change the answer to a percent.

Use These Steps

What is the percent of decrease from $20 to $15?

1. Subtract the new price from the old price to find the change in price.

    $20 − $15 = $5

2. Divide the change in price by the old price.

    $5 ÷ $20 = .25

3. Change to a percent.

    .25 = 25%

Find the percent of decrease.

	old price	new price	change in price	% of decrease
1.	$ 50	$ 45	$50 − $45 = $5	$5 ÷ $50 = .1 = 10%
2.	$ 20	$ 15		
3.	$120	$110		
4.	$ 36	$ 30		
5.	$ 75	$ 60		
6.	$ 10	$ 8		
7.	$100	$ 50		
8.	$ 6	$ 4		

Unit 5 *Review*

Find the part using a percent sentence.

1.
What is 27% of 200?

2.
What is $12\frac{1}{2}$% of 80?

3.
What is $2\frac{1}{2}$% of 400?

4.
What is 110% of 90?

Find the part using a proportion.

5.
What is 30% of 50?

6.
What is 25% of 80?

7.
What is 5% of 60?

8.
What is $33\frac{1}{3}$% of 60?

Find the whole using a percent sentence.

9.
15 is 3% of what number?

10.
21 is 14% of what number?

11.
8 is $12\frac{1}{2}$% of what number?

12.
44 is $4\frac{2}{5}$% of what number?

Find the whole using a proportion.

13.

45 is 50% of what number?

14.

9 is 300% of what number?

15.

90 is $33\frac{1}{3}$% of what number?

16.

40 is $66\frac{2}{3}$% of what number?

Find the percent using a percent sentence.

17.

19 is what percent of 500?

18.

27 is what percent of 108?

19.

25 is what percent of 150?

20.

21 is what percent of 240?

Find the percent using a proportion.

21.

13 is what percent of 26?

22.

120 is what percent of 1,200?

23.

80 is what percent of 320?

24.

6 is what percent of 30?

Find the percent of increase or decrease.

	old	new	change in price	% of increase or decrease
25.	$ 50	$ 55		
26.	$ 30	$ 25		
27.	$ 16	$ 18		
28.	$ 5	$ 4		
29.	$ 25	$ 15		
30.	$ 60	$ 70		
31.	$150	$120		
32.	$ 40	$ 30		
33.	$180	$240		
34.	$ 75	$150		

Below is a list of the problems in this review and the pages on which the skills are taught. If you missed any problems, turn to the pages listed and practice the skills. Then correct the problems you missed in the Unit Review.

You have studied decimals, ratios, proportions, and percents. You have applied these skills to real-life problems, and you have learned techniques for solving word problems.

In this unit, you will learn how to choose the correct operation needed to solve problems. You will also learn how to solve problems that require you to use more than one operation to find the answers.

Getting Ready

You should be familiar with the skills on this page and the next before you begin this unit.

 When adding and subtracting decimals, line up the decimal points. Add zeros and decimal points if necessary.

Add or subtract.

1.	2.	3.	4.
$1.2 + 4.72 =$	$12.6 + .02 =$	$213.7 + 6.98 =$	$85.06 + .04 =$

$$\begin{array}{r} 1.20 \\ +\ 4.72 \\ \hline 5.92 \end{array}$$

5.	6.	7.	8.
$947.6 - 82.9 =$	$14 - 1.03 =$	$72.3 - 41.91 =$	$493.1 - .036 =$

When multiplying and dividing decimals, be sure to include a decimal point in the answer.

Multiply or divide.

9.

$1.3 \times 3 =$

$$
\begin{array}{r}
1.3 \\
\times\ \ 3 \\
\hline
3.9
\end{array}
$$

10.

$.03 \times .07 =$

11.

$12.72 \div 8 =$

12.

$71.04 \div 32 =$

For review, see Unit 3.

 Sometimes it is necessary to change a percent to a decimal or a fraction before solving a problem.

Change each percent to a decimal and a fraction. Reduce if possible.

13.

$50\% = .50 = \frac{1}{2}$

14.

$2\% =$

15.

$25\% =$

16.

$33\frac{1}{3}\% =$

17.

$670\% =$

18.

$16\frac{2}{3}\% =$

For review, see Unit 4.

You can find the missing piece in a percent problem by using a percent sentence: part = whole $\times$ percent.

Find the part, the whole, and the percent.

19.

What is 50% of 40?
whole = 40
percent = 50% = .5
part = 40 $\times$ .5 = 20

20.

What is $33\frac{1}{3}\%$ of 90?

21.

16 is 25% of what?

22.

100 is what percent of 500?

For review, see Unit 5.

Choose an Operation: Being a Consumer

If you have a savings account, you work with decimals all the time. Each time you make a deposit, you add the amount of the deposit to your balance. Each time you withdraw money from your account, you subtract the amount of the withdrawal from your balance. And when the bank pays you interest, you add that amount to your balance.

Example On January 1, the balance in Vanessa's savings account was $356.89. On payday, January 15, she deposited $37. What was her new balance after she made the deposit?

▶ **Step 1.** To find her new balance, add her deposit to her old balance from January 1.

$$\begin{array}{r} \$356.89 \\ +\quad 37.00 \\ \hline \$393.89 \end{array}$$

Date	Withdrawal	Deposit	Interest Credited	Balance
Jan. 1				356 89
Jan. 15		37 00		393 89
Jan. 31				
Feb. 10	188 23			207 30
Feb. 15				
Feb. 16		450 00		581 80
Feb. 27	525 77			56 03
Feb. 28				
March 15		442 01		500 00
March 21				

▶ **Step 2.** Write her new balance in the last column on the same line in her bankbook as her deposit.

Vanessa's balance on January 15 was $393.89.

Find the balance in Vanessa's savings account. Write your answers in her bankbook.

1. On January 31, the bank paid Vanessa $1.64 in interest. What was her new balance on January 31?

2. On February 15 Vanessa had a balance of $207.30. She took out $75.50. What was her new balance?

Answer_____

Answer_____

3. On February 28, Vanessa had a balance of $56.03. The bank paid Vanessa $1.96 in interest. Circle the expression you would use to find Vanessa's new balance.
   a. $56.03 − $1.96   Solve for the
   b. $56.03 + $1.96   answer.
   c. $56.03 × $1.96
   d. $56.03 ÷ $1.96

4. On March 21, Vanessa had a balance of $500.00. She took out $234.75. Circle the expression you would use to find Vanessa's new balance.
   a. $500.00 − $234.75   Solve for the
   b. $500.00 + $234.75   answer.
   c. $500.00 × $234.75
   d. $500.00 ÷ $234.75

Answer_____

Answer_____

Choose an Operation: Using Data Analysis

After a basketball game, newspapers list the top players, the number of games they played, and the number of points they scored. To find a player's average score, sports writers divide the number of points the player scored by the number of games the player played. They round the answer to the nearest tenth.

Example Gordon has played in 44 games this season. He has scored 1,305 points. How many points did Gordon score per game?

▶ **Step 1.**   1,305 ÷ 44 = 29.65

▶ **Step 2.**   29.65 rounded to the nearest tenth is 29.7.

Gordon averaged 29.7 points per game.

Solve.

1. Williams played in 42 games. He scored 1,192 points. What is his average score in a game? Round the answer to the nearest tenth.

    Answer_____

2. Maulins played in 39 games. He averaged 26.9 points per game. How many total points did he score? Round the answer to the nearest whole number.

    Answer_____

3. Wing played in 42 games. He scored 1,003 points. Circle the expression you would use to find his average score. Round the answer to the nearest tenth.
    a. 1,003 + 42   Solve for the answer.
    b. 1,003 − 42
    c. 1,003 × 42
    d. 1,003 ÷ 42

    Answer_____

4. Hardy played in 39 games. He averaged 23.4 points per game. Circle the expression you would use to find the total points he scored. Round the answer to the nearest whole number.
    a. 23.4 + 39   Solve for the answer.
    b. 23.4 − 39
    c. 23.4 × 39
    d. 23.4 ÷ 39

    Answer_____

Choose an Operation: Changing Units of Measurement

Sometimes when we measure, we use the metric system. In the metric system, weight is measured in grams and length is measured in meters. 454 grams is equal to about 1 pound. One meter is equal to about 39 inches. Grams and meters are base units. Large weights are measured in kilograms. Long distances are measured in kilometers.

To change from one unit of measurement to another, remember that when you change from a small unit to a larger unit, you divide. When you change from a large unit to a smaller unit, you multiply.

> 1,000 meters = 1 kilometer
> 1,000 grams = 1 kilogram

Example   Mr. Wyatt bought 1,200 grams of fertilizer for his garden. How many kilograms are in 1,200 grams?

Step 1.   You are changing from a small unit (grams) to a larger unit (kilograms). You will need to divide.

Step 2.   Use the chart to find out how many grams are in one kilogram.

$$1,000 \text{ grams} = 1 \text{ kilogram}$$

Step 3.   Divide. $1,200 \div 1,000 = 1,200 = 1.2$

There are 1.2 kilograms in 1,200 grams.

Solve.

1. Tim stocks shelves at the supermarket. A large box of detergent that he is shelving weighs .3 kilograms. How many grams are in .3 kilograms?

    Answer_____

2. It is 2.1 kilometers from Ed's house to his school. How many meters are in 2.1 kilometers?

    Answer_____

3. Estella walks 500 meters to school each morning. Circle the expression you would use to find how many kilometers she walks.
    a. $500 \times 1,000$ Solve for the answer.
    b. $500 - 1,000$
    c. $500 \div 1,000$
    d. $500 + 1,000$

    Answer_____

4. A gardener has a box of wood chips that weighs 7,352 grams. Circle the expression you would use to find how many kilograms are in 7,352 grams.
    a. $7,352 \times 1,000$ Solve for the answer.
    b. $7,352 - 1,000$
    c. $7,352 \div 1,000$
    d. $7,352 + 1,000$

    Answer_____

Multi-Step Problems: Using Decimals and Percents

People who work in or own a store may need to find the total cost of a purchase after computing the sales tax. They may also need to figure out the sale price of merchandise. Both types of problems require finding a percent and then finding a total amount.

Example Mrs. Dawson needs to find the total cost of a customer's purchase. The customer has $25.22 in merchandise. If 7.5% sales tax is added, what is the total cost of the purchase?

▶ **Step 1.** Find the sales tax by multiplying the cost of the merchandise by the sales tax rate. Change the percent to a decimal before multiplying.

$$7.5\% = .075$$
$$\$25.22 \times .075 = \$1.8915$$
$$\$1.8915 \text{ rounds to } \$1.89$$

▶ **Step 2.** Add the amount of sales tax to the cost of the merchandise.

$$\begin{array}{r} \$25.22 \\ +\quad 1.89 \\ \hline \$27.11 \end{array}$$

The total cost is $27.11.

Solve each problem. Round the answer to the nearest hundredth, or cent.

1. Chris made purchases worth $235.56. If the sales tax rate is 6%, what is the total cost of the purchases?

2. The total cost, including tax, of a $20 mouse for a personal computer is $21. What is the sales tax rate?

Answer_____   Answer_____

3. Ms. Keats made a monthly payment of $150 on a computer she bought for her home. If 15% of the payment was interest and the rest went toward paying off the balance, how much money went toward paying off her balance?

Answer_____

4. Rex Jewelry Shop charges its customers 1.5% per month interest on any unpaid balance. A customer has an unpaid balance of $45.90. How much will the customer pay next month if she pays off her balance plus one month's interest?

Answer_____

5. For the clearance sale at Blacks, Mr. Yian is marking down prices of sporting equipment by 30%. If the original price of a soccer ball was $40, what is the sale price?

Answer_____

6. If knee pads are being marked down by 25%, what was the original cost of those that now sell for $15?

Answer_____

7. Edna made a payment of $10 which included a finance charge of $3.89. What percent of her payment went for the finance charge?

Answer_____

8. What percent of Edna's payment went to pay off her balance?

Answer_____

9. On his lunch break, Troy ate at a Chinese restaurant. His meal cost $6.25. If the sales tax is 8% and he leaves a 15% tip, what will the total cost of his lunch be?

Answer_____

10. Hisako sold a poster that originally cost $5.99 for $4.10. What was the percent of discount on the poster? Round to the nearest whole percent.

Answer_____

Multi-Step Problems: Using Measurement

You can figure out how far you have gone (distance) if you know how fast you are going (rate) and how long it will take you to get from one place to another (time). The distance formula below shows you how.

distance (D) = rate (R) × time (T)

If you want to find the rate, use this formula:

rate (R) = distance (D) ÷ time (T)

If you want to find the time, use this formula:

time (T) = distance (D) ÷ rate (R)

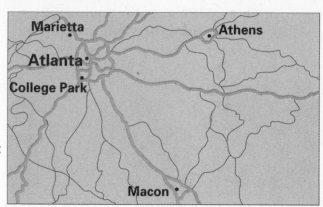

Always show time as a decimal or as a fraction of an hour.

Example How long will it take to drive 275 miles if you travel an average of 50 miles per hour?

▶ **Step 1.** Since you are looking for time, use the time formula.

$$T = D ÷ R$$

▶ **Step 2.** Substitute the numbers in the formula. Solve by dividing.

$$T = 275 ÷ 50 = 5.5 \text{ or } 5\frac{1}{2} \text{ hours}$$

It will take 5.5 or $5\frac{1}{2}$ hours.

Solve.

1. Mr. Cortez is driving to a new construction site. He needs to travel 30 miles in 45 minutes. How many miles per hour will he travel?

2. The speed limit on one stretch of Sunset Highway is 60 miles per hour. How far can you travel at this rate in 4 hours and 30 minutes?

Answer_____

Answer_____

Solve.

3. April Martin and her mother are traveling 300 miles to Atlanta. How long will it take them to get to Atlanta if they drive 60 miles per hour?

Answer_____

4. April found out that she and her mother can fly to Atlanta in 45 minutes. How many miles per hour will the plane travel?

Answer_____

5. Mrs. Martin found out that a bus averages 50 miles per hour. If they take the bus, how much longer will it take April and Mrs. Martin to get to Atlanta than if they take a plane? Write the answer using hours.

Answer_____

6. Normally Mr. Yang can make the 75-mile trip to Houston in 1 hour and 15 minutes. What is his usual rate of speed for the trip?

Answer_____

7. On his last trip to Houston, Mr. Yang had to take a detour. He averaged 30 miles per hour. How long did it take him to drive the 75 miles to Houston? Write the answer using hours.

Answer_____

8. The speed limit on the detour was 35 miles per hour. Mr. Yang drove for 30 minutes at this rate. How long was the detour?

Answer_____

9. The speed limit on Scenic Highway is 55 miles per hour. Next year the speed limit will be raised to 65 miles per hour. How much farther will you be able to travel in 2 hours next year?

Answer_____

10. Due to construction, the speed limit on a stretch of Scenic Highway has been reduced to 30 miles per hour. How far can you travel in 2 hours?

Answer_____

Multi-Step Problems: Using Data Analysis

Suppose that the federal government spends about 1,252 billion dollars yearly. The circle graph shows what percent of the total amount is spent in each area.

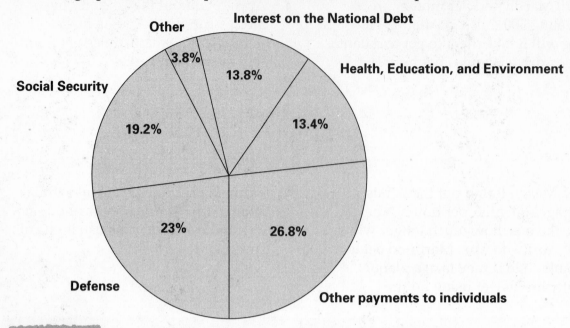

Example How much money does the federal government spend on interest on the national debt?

▶ **Step 1.** Find the percent spent on interest on the national debt in the graph and write a proportion.

$$\frac{n}{\$1,252} = \frac{13.8}{100}$$

▶ **Step 2.** Cross-multiply. Round to the nearest tenth.

$$n \times 100 = \$1,252 \times 13.8$$
$$100\,n = \$17,277.6$$
$$n = \$17,277.6 \div 100$$
$$n = \$172.776$$

$172.776 rounded to the nearest tenth is $172.8.

The federal government spent 172.8 billion dollars on interest on the national debt.

Solve. Round the answer to the nearest tenth.

1. How much money does the federal government spend on Social Security?

2. How much money does the federal government spend on defense?

Answer_____   Answer_____

3. How much money does the federal government spend on health, education, and the environment?

Answer_____

4. How much money does the federal government spend on other payments to individuals?

Answer_____

5. The federal government spends 1% of the budget on science, space, and technology. How much money is 1% of the federal budget?

Answer_____

6. Veterans benefits are 2.3% of the total budget. How much money does the federal government spend on veterans benefits?

Answer_____

7. The federal government spends 150 billion dollars on welfare payments. What percent of the total budget is this?

Answer_____

8. The federal government spends 100 billion dollars on Medicare. What percent of the total budget is this?

Answer_____

9. The federal government spends 17 billion dollars on the environment. What percent of the total budget is this?

Answer_____

10. The federal government spends 60 billion dollars on education. What percent of the total budget is this?

Answer_____

11. If the federal government spent only 12% on defense, how much money would it spend?

Answer_____

12. If interest on the national debt increased to 27.6%, how much money would the federal government spend on interest?

Answer_____

Decimals and Percents Skills Inventory

Write as a decimal.

1. two hundredths   2. four and one fourth   3. three dollars   4. six cents

Change to a decimal.

5. $\frac{3}{4} =$ 6. $\frac{1}{3} =$ 7. $\frac{1}{10} =$ 8. $4\frac{3}{5} =$

Change to a mixed number or fraction. Reduce if possible.

9. .8 =   10. .03 =   11. 1.75 =   12. 18.91 =

Compare. Write <, >, or = in each box.

13. .2 ☐ .200   14. 2.05 ☐ 2.5   15. .39 ☐ .30   16. 2.6 ☐ 6.2

Round to the nearest whole number.

17. 2.4 _____   18. .7 _____   19. 6.52 _____   20. 8.1 _____

Round to the nearest tenth.

21. 6.39 _____   22. .84 _____   23. .311 _____   24. 23.45 _____

Round to the nearest hundredth.

25. .357 _____   26. .036 _____   27. 4.298 _____   28. 4.3261 _____

Add, subtract, multiply, or divide. Round division answers to the nearest hundredth.

29.	30.	31.	32.	33.
$5.83 + 6.75	36.45 + 27.9	$4.00 − 1.97	37.2 − 4.065	10 − 4.32

34.	35.	36.	37.	38.
$8.67 × 5	$ .33 × 100	3.69 × 4.7	9.324 × .09	.3 × .2

39.
$$4)\overline{\$83.80}$$

40.
$$18)\overline{\$8.90}$$

41.
$$10)\overline{\$.80}$$

42.
$$.5)\overline{.12}$$

43.
$$1.3)\overline{2.49}$$

Write a ratio.

44. 7 runs in 5 innings **45.** 3 out of 6 doctors **46.** 3 pitches and 3 strikes

Solve each proportion.

47. $\frac{4}{6} = \frac{n}{3}$ **48.** $\frac{1}{3} = \frac{4}{n}$ **49.** $\frac{n}{7} = \frac{2}{14}$ **50.** $\frac{4}{n} = \frac{1}{2}$

Write a percent using the percent sign.

51. three percent =

52. four and one half percent =

Change to a decimal or a percent.

53. 30% = **54.** 106% = **55.** $3\frac{1}{2}\% =$ **56.** $66\frac{2}{3}\% =$

57. .09 = **58.** .4 = **59.** .25 = **60.** 4 =

Change to a whole number or a fraction. Reduce if necessary.

61. 50% = **62.** 8% = **63.** 200% = **64.** $3\frac{1}{4}\% =$

Change to a percent.

65. $\frac{1}{4} =$ **66.** $\frac{6}{100} =$ **67.** $\frac{5}{6} =$ **68.** $\frac{1}{5} =$

Compare. Use <, >, or = sign.

69.
.5 ☐ 50%

70.
90% ☐ 9

71.
$\frac{1}{4}$ ☐ 4%

72.
$16\frac{2}{3}$% ☐ $\frac{1}{6}$

Solve.

73.
What is 2% of 60?

74.
What is $66\frac{2}{3}$% of 90?

75.
What is 150% of 20?

76.
5 is 20% of what?

77.
30 is 300% of what number?

78.
125 is $1\frac{1}{4}$% of what number?

79.
15 is what percent of 80?

80.
99 is what percent of 33?

Below is a list of the problems in this Skills Inventory and the pages on which the skills are taught. If you missed any problems, turn to the pages listed and practice the skills. Then correct the problems you missed in the Skills Inventory.

Problem	Practice Page	Problem	Practice Page	Problem	Practice Page
Unit 1		*Unit 2*		53-56	82-84
1-2	13-14	29-30	33-36	57-60	86
3-4	17	31-33	39-42	61-64	90-91
5-8	11-12, 21-22	*Unit 3*		65-68	92-93
9-12	16	34-38	49-56	69-72	95-96
13-16	20, 23	39-43	59-68	*Unit 5*	
17-20	25	*Unit 4*		73-75	107-111, 115-116, 119
21-24	26	44-46	75	76-78	122-125, 127-128
25-28	27	47-50	76-78	79-80	131-133, 135
		51-52	81		

Glossary

addition (page 31) - Putting numbers together to find a total. The symbol + is used in addition.

$$\begin{array}{r} 1.43 \\ + \ 6.12 \\ \hline 7.55 \end{array}$$

average (page 89) - The amount you get when you divide a total by the number of items you added to get that total.

$$\left.\begin{array}{r} 3.2 \\ 4.7 \\ + \ 2. \\ \hline 9.9 \end{array}\right\} 3 \text{ items}$$

$$\begin{array}{r} 3.3 \\ 3\overline{)9.9} \end{array}$$

borrowing (page 32) - Taking an amount from a top digit in subtraction and adding it to the next digit to the right.

$$\begin{array}{r} ^{114} \\ 3.\cancel{2}4 \\ - \ 1.07 \\ \hline 2.17 \end{array}$$

carrying (page 32) - Taking an amount from the sum of digits with the same place value and adding it to the next column of digits to the left.

$$\begin{array}{r} ^{1} \\ 3.29 \\ + \ 1.24 \\ \hline 4.53 \end{array}$$

chart (page 94) - Information arranged in rows and columns.

ITEM	NUMBER SOLD	COST
Rulers	8	$ 8.00
Scissors	2	1.68
Pencils	16	.48
Staplers	4	12.40
Pens	12	9.48
Notepads	6	2.70
TOTAL	48	$34.74

circle graph (page 150) - A circle cut into sections to show the parts that make a total.

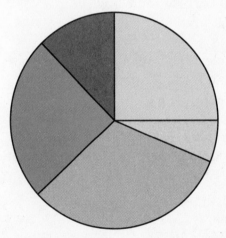

column (page 43) - A vertical line of numbers.

3 2 9
5 4 1
0 6 7

comparing (page 23) - Deciding if a number is equal to, greater than, or less than another number.

complex percent (page 84) - A percent that has a whole number and a fraction.

$33\frac{1}{3}\%$

cross-multiplying (page 76) - Multiplying the numbers on opposite corners of a proportion.

$\frac{1}{3} \bowtie \frac{n}{15}$

$3 \times n = 1 \times 15$

$3n = 15$

$n = 5$

decimal (page 9) - A number or part of a number that is less than 1.

.13   6.42

decimal point (page 11) - A decimal point separates the whole number and decimal part of a decimal.

1.2

denominator (page 10) - The bottom number in a fraction. The number of equal parts in the whole.

$\frac{2}{3}$

digit (page 13) - One of the ten symbols used to write numbers.

0 1 2 3 4 5 6 7 8 9

division (page 21) - Splitting an amount into equal groups. The symbols ÷ and ⟌ are used in division.

$1.2 \div 2 = .6$ $2\overline{)1.2}$ = .6

equal (page 20) - The same in value. The symbol = means *equal*.

$6 = 6.0$

equivalent (page 84) - The same in value.

$1\frac{1}{2}\% = .015\%$

estimating (page 69) - Finding an answer by rounding the numbers in a problem. You use estimating when an exact answer is not needed.

formula (page 113) - A mathematical sentence that uses letters to show a relationship.

I = prt

fraction (page 9) - Part of a whole or a group.

$\frac{3}{10}$

fraction bar (page 21) - The line that separates the numerator and denominator of a fraction.

$\frac{2}{3}$

greater than (page 23) - More than. The symbol > means *greater than*.

1 > .1 means 1 is greater than .1

higher terms (page 10) - A fraction is in higher terms when you multiply the numerator and denominator by the same number.

$\frac{1}{2} = \frac{1 \times 2}{2 \times 2} = \frac{2}{4}$

hundredth (page 14) - A decimal with two places to the right of the decimal point.

two hundredths = .02

improper fraction (page 90) - A fraction with the numerator equal to or larger than the denominator.

$\frac{4}{4}$ $\frac{7}{4}$

invert (page 124) - Turn upside down.

$\frac{1}{2} \bowtie \frac{2}{1}$

less than (page 23) - Smaller than. The symbol < means *less than*.

.1 < 1 means .1 is less than 1

lowest terms (page 10) - A fraction is in lowest terms when 1 is the only number that divides evenly into both the numerator and the denominator.
$$\frac{4}{8} = \frac{4 \div 4}{8 \div 4} = \frac{1}{2}$$

minus (page 118) - To subtract. The symbol for minus is − .

mixed number (page 11) - A number with a whole number part and a fraction part.
$$2\frac{1}{2}$$

multiplication (page 12) - Combining equal numbers two or more times to get a total. The symbol × is used in multiplication.

$$\begin{array}{r} 4 \\ 4.7 \\ \times\ \ 6 \\ \hline 28.2 \end{array}$$

n (page 77) - A symbol used to stand for a missing number.

not equal (page 20) - Different in value. The symbol ≠ means *not equal*.
$$4.1 \neq 4.01$$

numerator (page 10) - The top number in a fraction. The number of parts being considered.
$$\frac{5}{9}$$

operation (page 141) - The process you use to solve a math problem. The basic operations are addition, subtraction, multiplication, and division.

partial product (page 51) - The total you get when you multiply a number by one digit of another number.

$$\begin{array}{r} 2.31 \\ \times\ \ 1.2 \\ \hline 462 \\ 2\ 31 \\ \hline 2.772 \end{array}$$

percent (page 73) - A percent is a part of something. The symbol % is used to show percent.

twenty-five percent = 25%

plus (page 32) - To add. The symbol for plus is +.

proportion (page 73) - Two equal ratios or fractions.
$$\frac{3}{4} = \frac{9}{12}$$

ratio (page 73) - A fraction showing the relationship of two numbers.

3 out of 4 doctors $\frac{3}{4}$

reducing (page 10) - Dividing both the numerator and denominator of a fraction by the same number.
$$\frac{6}{9} = \frac{6 \div 3}{9 \div 3} = \frac{2}{3}$$

remainder (page 22) - the numerator of a fraction when the amount left over in a division problem is shown as a fraction.

$$\begin{array}{r} .33\frac{1}{3} \\ 3)\overline{1.00} \\ -\ \ 9 \\ \hline 10 \\ -\ \ 9 \\ \hline 1 \end{array}$$

renaming (page 32) - Carrying or borrowing a number.

$$\begin{array}{r} \overset{1}{2.6} \\ + 1.9 \\ \hline 4.5 \end{array} \qquad \begin{array}{r} \overset{3\;16}{\cancel{4.6}} \\ - 1.9 \\ \hline 2.7 \end{array}$$

rounding (page 25) - Expressing a number to the nearest tenth, hundredth, thousandth, and so on.

row (page 51) - A horizontal line of numbers.

3 2 9
5 4 1
0 6 7

subtraction (page 31) - Taking away a certain amount from another amount to find a difference. The symbol − is used in subtraction.

$$\begin{array}{r} 7.5 \\ - 1.4 \\ \hline 6.1 \end{array}$$

table (page 43) - Information arranged in rows and columns.

ITEM	NUMBER SOLD	COST
Rulers	8	$ 8.00
Scissors	2	1.68
Pencils	16	.48
Staplers	4	12.40
Pens	12	9.48
Notepads	6	2.70
TOTAL	48	$34.74

ten thousandth (page 19) - A decimal with four places to the right of the decimal point.

eight ten thousandths = .0008

tenth (page 13) - A decimal with one place to the right of the decimal point.

four tenths = .4

thousandth (page 19) - A decimal with three places to the right of the decimal point.

forty-five thousandths = .045

whole number (page 9) - A number that shows a whole amount.

zero (page 16) - The word name for 0.

KEY OPERATION WORDS

Word problems often contain clue words that help you solve the problem. These words tell you whether you need to add, subtract, multiply, or divide. The lists of words below will help you decide which operation to use when solving word problems.

Addition

add
all together
and
both
combined
in all
increase
more
plus
sum
total

Subtraction

change (money)
decrease
difference
left
less than
more than
reduce
remain or remaining
smaller, larger, farther,
     nearer, and so on

Multiplication

in all
of
multiply
product
times (as much)
total
twice
whole

Division

average
cut
divide
each
equal pieces
every
one
split

TABLE OF MEASUREMENTS

Time

60 seconds = 1 minute
60 minutes = 1 hour
24 hours = 1 day
7 days = 1 week
52 weeks = 1 year
12 months = 1 year
365 days = 1 year

Weight

16 ounces = 1 pound
2,000 pounds = 1 ton

Length

12 inches = 1 foot
36 inches = 1 yard
3 feet = 1 yard
5,280 feet = 1 mile
1,760 yards = 1 mile

Capacity

8 ounces = 1 cup
2 cups = 1 pint
4 cups = 1 quart
2 pints = 1 quart
4 quarts = 1 gallon
8 pints = 1 gallon
16 cups = 1 gallon

EQUIVALENT FRACTIONS, DECIMALS, AND PERCENTS

Fraction	Decimal	Percent
$\frac{1}{2}$	.5	50%
$\frac{2}{2} = 1$	1.0	100%

Fraction	Decimal	Percent
$\frac{1}{3}$	$.33\frac{1}{3}$	$33\frac{1}{3}\%$
$\frac{2}{3}$	$.66\frac{2}{3}$	$66\frac{2}{3}\%$
$\frac{3}{3} = 1$	1.0	100%

Fraction	Decimal	Percent
$\frac{1}{4}$	.25	25%
$\frac{2}{4} = \frac{1}{2}$	.5	50%
$\frac{3}{4}$	.75	75%
$\frac{4}{4} = 1$	1.0	100%

Fraction	Decimal	Percent
$\frac{1}{5}$	.2	20%
$\frac{2}{5}$	.4	40%
$\frac{3}{5}$	.6	60%
$\frac{4}{5}$	.8	80%
$\frac{5}{5} = 1$	1.0	100%

Fraction	Decimal	Percent
$\frac{1}{6}$	$.16\frac{2}{3}$	$16\frac{2}{3}\%$
$\frac{2}{6} = \frac{1}{3}$	$.33\frac{1}{3}$	$33\frac{1}{3}\%$
$\frac{3}{6} = \frac{1}{2}$	.5	50%
$\frac{4}{6} = \frac{2}{3}$	$.66\frac{2}{3}$	$66\frac{2}{3}\%$
$\frac{5}{6}$	$.83\frac{1}{3}$	$83\frac{1}{3}\%$
$\frac{6}{6} = 1$	1.0	100%

Fraction	Decimal	Percent
$\frac{1}{8}$	.125	$12\frac{1}{2}\%$
$\frac{2}{8} = \frac{1}{4}$	.25	25%
$\frac{3}{8}$	$.37\frac{1}{2}$	$37\frac{1}{2}\%$
$\frac{4}{8} = \frac{1}{2}$	.5	50%
$\frac{5}{8}$	$.62\frac{1}{2}$	$62\frac{1}{2}\%$
$\frac{6}{8} = \frac{3}{4}$	.75	75%
$\frac{7}{8}$	$.87\frac{1}{2}$	$87\frac{1}{2}\%$
$\frac{8}{8} = 1$	1.0	100%

Fraction	Decimal	Percent
$\frac{1}{10}$	.1	10%
$\frac{2}{10} = \frac{1}{5}$	.2	20%
$\frac{3}{10}$	.3	30%
$\frac{4}{10} = \frac{2}{5}$	.4	40%
$\frac{5}{10} = \frac{1}{2}$	.5	50%
$\frac{6}{10} = \frac{3}{5}$	.6	60%
$\frac{7}{10}$	.7	70%
$\frac{8}{10} = \frac{4}{5}$	.8	80%
$\frac{9}{10}$	.9	90%
$\frac{10}{10} = 1$	1.0	100%

Fraction	Decimal	Percent
$\frac{1}{100}$	.01	1%
1	1.0	100%

THE PERCENT TRIANGLE

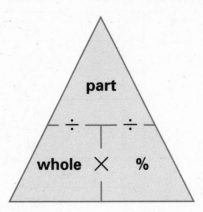

To solve for the part, cover the word *part*. The remaining pieces are connected by a multiplication sign. Multiply the pieces you have to find the part.

part = whole × percent

To solve for the whole, cover the word *whole*. The remaining pieces are connected by a division sign. Divide the pieces you have to find the whole.

whole = part ÷ percent

To solve for the percent, cover the percent sign. The remaining pieces are connected by a division sign. Divide the pieces you have to find the percent.

percent = part ÷ whole

Addition Facts Table

+	0	1	2	3	4	5	6	7	8	9
0	0	1	2	3	4	5	6	7	8	9
1	1	2	3	4	5	6	7	8	9	10
2	2	3	4	5	6	7	8	9	10	11
3	3	4	5	6	7	8	9	10	11	12
4	4	5	6	7	8	9	10	11	12	13
5	5	6	7	8	9	10	11	12	13	14
6	6	7	8	9	10	11	12	13	14	15
7	7	8	9	10	11	12	13	14	15	16
8	8	9	10	11	12	13	14	15	16	17
9	9	10	11	12	13	14	15	16	17	18

Subtraction Facts Table

−	0	1	2	3	4	5	6	7	8	9
0	0	1	2	3	4	5	6	7	8	9
1	1	2	3	4	5	6	7	8	9	10
2	2	3	4	5	6	7	8	9	10	11
3	3	4	5	6	7	8	9	10	11	12
4	4	5	6	7	8	9	10	11	12	13
5	5	6	7	8	9	10	11	12	13	14
6	6	7	8	9	10	11	12	13	14	15
7	7	8	9	10	11	12	13	14	15	16
8	8	9	10	11	12	13	14	15	16	17
9	9	10	11	12	13	14	15	16	17	18

Multiplication Facts Table

×	0	1	2	3	4	5	6	7	8	9
0	0	0	0	0	0	0	0	0	0	0
1	0	1	2	3	4	5	6	7	8	9
2	0	2	4	6	8	10	12	14	16	18
3	0	3	6	9	12	15	18	21	24	27
4	0	4	8	12	16	20	24	28	32	36
5	0	5	10	15	20	25	30	35	40	45
6	0	6	12	18	24	30	36	42	48	54
7	0	7	14	21	28	35	42	49	56	63
8	0	8	16	24	32	40	48	56	64	72
9	0	9	18	27	36	45	54	63	72	81

Division Facts Table

÷	0	1	2	3	4	5	6	7	8	9
1	0	1	2	3	4	5	6	7	8	9
2	0	2	4	6	8	10	12	14	16	18
3	0	3	6	9	12	15	18	21	24	27
4	0	4	8	12	16	20	24	28	32	36
5	0	5	10	15	20	25	30	35	40	45
6	0	6	12	18	24	30	36	42	48	54
7	0	7	14	21	28	35	42	49	56	63
8	0	8	16	24	32	40	48	56	64	72
9	0	9	18	27	36	45	54	63	72	81